What Is Seen
and
What Is NOT Seen

Fun Systems Thinking Activities *with* Frédéric Bastiat
Supplementary Economics Activity Book to *Systems Thinking Basics*

by Michael Frederick Reber

The Frédéric Bastiat
Systems Thinking Series *in*
Political Economy
Book 1

Permission granted by the Foundation for Economic Education (FEE) to re-print Frédéric Bastiat's *What Is Seen and What Is Not Seen*. The full downloadable version of Bastiat's work can be obtained from the FEE website at http://fee.org/doc/selected_essays_on_politcal_economy/

Permission granted by Pegasus Communications to quote and summarize material in *Systems Thinking Basics*.

"What is Seen and What is Not Seen: Fun Systems Thinking Activities with Frédéric Bastiat. Supplementary Economics Activity Book to Systems Thinking Basics," by Michael Frederick Reber. ISBN 978-1-60264-689-6.

Published 2011 by Virtualbookworm.com Publishing Inc., P.O. Box 9949, College Station, TX 77842, US. ©2011, Michael Frederick Reber. All rights reserved. No part of this publication may be reproduced, stored in a retrieval system, or transmitted in any form or by any means, electronic, mechanical, recording or otherwise, without the prior written permission of Michael Frederick Reber.

Manufactured in the United States of America.

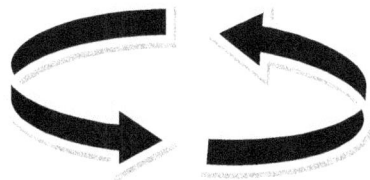

There is only one difference between a bad economist and a good one: the bad economist confines himself to the *visible* effect; the good economist takes into account both the effect that can be seen and those effects that must be *foreseen*.

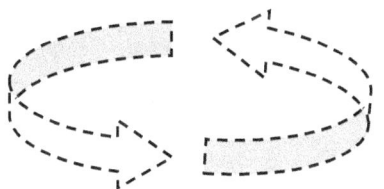

Frédéric Bastiat
July, 1850

Functional Table of Contents

Topics	Course Learning Outcomes ⊗	Unit Learning Outcomes ⊗	Activities ⊗	Assessment ⊗
To the Reader pp. i ~ xi				
Review pp. 1~10				
Systems Thinking Basics Review: • What is a system? • What is systems thinking? • What is a Behavior Over Time (BOT) Graph? • What is a Causal Loop Diagram (CLD)?	1. Demonstrate understanding of the concepts of a system 2. Demonstrate understanding of the levels of the perspective framework and how the levels relate to action modes 3. Demonstrate understanding of the concepts of systems thinking 4. Demonstrate understanding of systemic behavior	1. Demonstrate understanding of the characteristics of systems 2. Demonstrate understanding of the concept of feedback 3. Demonstrate understanding of the multiple levels of perspective and how they relate to action modes 4. Demonstrate understanding of the principles of systems thinking 5. Demonstrate understanding of BOT graphs 6. Demonstrate understanding of CLDs in general 7. Demonstrate understanding of reinforcing processes 8. Demonstrate understanding of balancing processes 9. Demonstrate understanding of balancing loops in their various aspects 10. Demonstrate understanding of delay in complex systems 11. Demonstrate understanding of physical delays in complex systems. 12. Demonstrate understanding of transactional delays 13. Demonstrate understanding of informational delays 14. Demonstrate understanding of perceptual delays 15. Demonstrate understanding of stocks and flows	Refer to *Systems Thinking Basics: From Concepts to Causal Loops*	Refer to *Systems Thinking Basics: From Concepts to Causal Loops*

Topics	Course Learning Outcomes	Unit Learning Outcomes	Activities	Assessment
Unit 1 pp. 12~21				
Systems Thinking with Frédéric Bastiat: The Broken Window	5. Demonstrate understanding of the free market system	1. Identify and explain the characteristics of the economic elements that Bastiat tells in his case of "The Broken Window" 2. Demonstrate understanding of the dynamics of the economic elements that Bastiat tells in his case of "The Broken Window"	Free writing → Information Gap Writing → Hands-On Activities: 1. Bastiat Activity 2. Real-World Activity → Journal Writing → Evaluation Notes →	Culturally-based presumptions New knowledge Experiential learning Reflection and synthesis Evaluation
Unit 2 pp. 22~30				
Systems Thinking with Frédéric Bastiat: The Demobilization	5. Demonstrate understanding of the free market system	1. Identify and explain the characteristics of the economic elements that Bastiat tells in his case of "The Demobilization" 2. Demonstrate understanding of the dynamics of the economic elements that Bastiat tells in his case of "The Demobilization"	Free writing → Information Gap Writing → Hands-On Activities: 1. Bastiat Activity 2. Real-World Activity → Journal Writing → Evaluation Notes →	Culturally-based presumptions New knowledge Experiential learning Reflection and synthesis Evaluation
Unit 3 pp. 31~40				
Systems Thinking with Frédéric Bastiat: Taxes	5. Demonstrate understanding of the free market system	1. Identify and explain the characteristics of the economic elements that Bastiat tells in his case of "Taxes" 2. Demonstrate understanding of the dynamics of the economic elements that Bastiat tells in his case of "Taxes"	Free writing → Information Gap Writing → Hands-On Activities: 1. Bastiat Activity 2. Real-World Activity → Journal Writing → Evaluation Notes →	Culturally-based presumptions New knowledge Experiential learning Reflection and synthesis Evaluation

Topics	Course Learning Outcomes	Unit Learning Outcomes	Activities	Assessment
Unit 4 pp. 41~51				
Systems Thinking with Frédéric Bastiat: Theaters and Fine Arts	5. Demonstrate understanding of the free market system	1. Identify and explain the characteristics of the economic elements that Bastiat tells in his case of "Theaters and Fine Arts" 2. Demonstrate understanding of the dynamics of the economic elements that Bastiat tells in his case of "Theaters and Fine Arts"	Free writing → Information Gap Writing → Hands-On Activities: 1. Bastiat Activity 2. Real-World Activity → Journal Writing → Evaluation Notes →	Culturally-based presumptions New knowledge Experiential learning Reflection and synthesis Evaluation
Unit 5 pp. 52~60				
Systems Thinking with Frédéric Bastiat: Public Works	5. Demonstrate understanding of the free market system	1. Identify and explain the characteristics of the economic elements that Bastiat tells in his case of "Public Works" 2. Demonstrate understanding of the dynamics of the economic elements that Bastiat tells in his case of "Public Works"	Free writing → Information Gap Writing → Hands-On Activities: 1. Bastiat Activity 2. Real-World Activity → Journal Writing → Evaluation Notes →	Culturally-based presumptions New knowledge Experiential learning Reflection and synthesis Evaluation
Unit 6 pp. 61~72				
Systems Thinking with Frédéric Bastiat: The Middlemen	5. Demonstrate understanding of the free market system	1. Identify and explain the characteristics of the economic elements that Bastiat tells in his case of "The Middlemen" 2. Demonstrate understanding of the dynamics of the economic elements that Bastiat tells in his case of "The Middlemen"	Free writing → Information Gap Writing → Hands-On Activities: 1. Bastiat Activity 2. Real-World Activity → Journal Writing → Evaluation Notes →	Culturally-based presumptions New knowledge Experiential learning Reflection and synthesis Evaluation

Topics	Course Learning Outcomes	Unit Learning Outcomes	Activities	Assessment
Unit 7 pp. 73~83				
Systems Thinking with Frédéric Bastiat: Restraint of Trade	5. Demonstrate understanding of the free market system	1. Identify and explain the characteristics of the economic elements that Bastiat tells in his case of "Restraint of Trade" 2. Demonstrate understanding of the dynamics of the economic elements that Bastiat tells in his case of "Restraint of Trade"	Free writing → Information Gap Writing → Hands-On Activities: 1. Bastiat Activity 2. Real-World Activity → Journal Writing → Evaluation Notes →	Culturally-based presumptions New knowledge Experiential learning Reflection and synthesis Evaluation
Unit 8 pp. 84~95				
Systems Thinking with Frédéric Bastiat: Machines	5. Demonstrate understanding of the free market system	1. Identify and explain the characteristics of the economic elements that Bastiat tells in his case of "Machines" 2. Demonstrate understanding of the dynamics of the economic elements that Bastiat tells in his case of "Machines"	Free writing → Information Gap Writing → Hands-On Activities: 1. Bastiat Activity 2. Real-World Activity → Journal Writing → Evaluation Notes →	Culturally-based presumptions New knowledge Experiential learning Reflection and synthesis Evaluation
Unit 9 pp. 96~105				
Systems Thinking with Frédéric Bastiat: Credit	5. Demonstrate understanding of the free market system	1. Identify and explain the characteristics of the economic elements that Bastiat tells in his case of "Credit" 2. Demonstrate understanding of the dynamics of the economic elements that Bastiat tells in his case of "Credit"	Free writing → Information Gap Writing → Hands-On Activities: 1. Bastiat Activity 2. Real-World Activity → Journal Writing → Evaluation Notes →	Culturally-based presumptions New knowledge Experiential learning Reflection and synthesis Evaluation

Topics	Course Learning Outcomes	Unit Learning Outcomes	Activities	Assessment
Unit 10 pp. 106~115				
Systems Thinking with Frédéric Bastiat: Algeria	5. Demonstrate understanding of the free market system	1. Identify and explain the characteristics of the economic elements that Bastiat tells in his case of "Algeria" 2. Demonstrate understanding of the dynamics of the economic elements that Bastiat tells in his case of "Algeria"	Free writing → Information Gap Writing → Hands-On Activities: 1. Bastiat Activity 2. Real-World Activity → Journal Writing → Evaluation Notes →	Culturally-based presumptions New knowledge Experiential learning Reflection and synthesis Evaluation
Unit 11 pp. 116~127				
Systems Thinking with Frédéric Bastiat: Thrift and Luxury	5. Demonstrate understanding of the free market system	1. Identify and explain the characteristics of the economic elements that Bastiat tells in his case of "Thrift and Luxury" 2. Demonstrate understanding of the dynamics of the economic elements that Bastiat tells in his case of "Thrift and Luxury"	Free writing → Information Gap Writing → Hands-On Activities: 1. Bastiat Activity 2. Real-World Activity → Journal Writing → Evaluation Notes →	Culturally-based presumptions New knowledge Experiential learning Reflection and synthesis Evaluation
Unit 12 pp. 128~136				
Systems Thinking with Frédéric Bastiat: The Right to Employment and the Right to Profit	5. Demonstrate understanding of the free market system	1. Identify and explain the characteristics of the economic elements that Bastiat tells in "The Right to Employment and the Right to Profit" 2. Demonstrate understanding of the dynamics of the economic elements that Bastiat tells in "The Right to Employment and the Right to Profit"	Free writing → Information Gap Writing → Hands-On Activities: 1. Bastiat Activity 2. Real-World Activity → Journal Writing → Evaluation Notes →	Culturally-based presumptions New knowledge Experiential learning Reflection and synthesis Evaluation

Appendix: Learning Activity Key Points and Suggested Responses, pp. 138~164

To The Reader

To The Reader

Welcome to the global economy!

That's right. We live in a complex, interrelated global economy which is becoming more interrelated and complex every day. So this means that to survive in this new economy, we all need to understand its systemic functions. And that means knowing how to think systemically. By using this activity book, you will learn to apply two foundational devices of systems thinking, *behavior over time (BOT) graphs* and *causal loop diagrams (CLDs)*, for understanding the global economy, or more specifically, the international free market system.

Why Systems Thinking?

Economic systems are social systems just like any of our other social systems, such as educational or political systems. But what makes economic systems, or more exactly, free market economic systems, so unique is that they are perhaps the most ubiquitous of all our social systems. Every day we see more regional and national economic systems integrate into the global free market economy which in turn makes our lives and our social systems more inter-related and complex. As we saw with the US financial crisis in 2008 and 2009, whatever happened on the New York Stock Exchange had great effects on the daily lives of people in Iceland, Greece, Spain, and many other places around the world. So, to truly understand economics, you have to understand systems thinking. As Virginia Anderson and Lauren Keller Johnson state in *Systems Thinking Basics*, "One of the major points that systems thinking makes is that everything—and everyone—is interconnected in an infinitely complex network of systems." You will learn more about the importance of systems thinking for understanding economics as you read Frédéric Bastiat's *What Is Seen and What Is Not Seen* throughout this activity book.

How to Use This Book

What Is Seen and What Is Not Seen: Fun Systems Thinking Activities with Frédéric Bastiat is a supplementary activity book to Virginia Anderson and Lauren Keller Johnson's *Systems Thinking Basics: From Concepts to Causal Loops*. It is specifically designed for economics students or anyone interested in economics, and applies the systems thinking concepts and tools in *Systems Thinking Basics*. Therefore, it is highly recommended that you do *Systems Thinking Basics* before or in conjunction with this activity book.

The systems thinking praxis of this activity book is unique. No other systems thinking book on the market applies in an engaging and fun way Frédéric Bastiat's seminal work in economic thought, *What Is Seen and What Is Not Seen*. Furthermore, Bastiat's writing is simple and to the point and this makes using systems thinking for economics easy and fun. As the 1974 Nobel Prize Winner in Economics, F.A. Hayek, declares about Bastiat's work, "No one has ever stated more clearly...the central difficulty of a rational economic policy."

Another unique quality of this book is its "functional" table of contents. This means it shows learning alignment: topics, course learning outcomes, unit learning outcomes, activities, and assessment are all explicit. It is designed to be very simple and clear in order for you to know what is to be learned, why it is to be learned, and how your learning is to be assessed.

After looking at the table of contents, go directly to the unit. Each unit is broken up according to the Experiential Learning Approach (ELA). It assists you with using your critical and systemic thinking skills via the cyclical process of articulating presumptions through free-writing and discussion, acquiring and understanding new knowledge by attending lectures and collecting data, engaging in experiential learning exercises through critical thinking activities, reflecting on your learning and synthesizing new ideas and concepts through journal and essay writing, and evaluating your learning through self-reflection and teacher-peer feedback.

"Experiential Learning Approach (ELA)"

```
    Culturally-based  ──────▶  New
    Presumptions              Knowledge
        ▲                         │
        │                         ▼
    Evaluation              Experiential
        ▲                    Learning
        │                         │
    Reflection and  ◀─────────────┘
     Synthesis
```

1. <u>Culturally-based Presumptions</u>: Record in your journal your current understandings of the vital issue being addressed before engaging in the new learning experience.
2. <u>New Knowledge</u>: Acquire new knowledge about the vital issue being addressed by attending lectures and gathering data on the issue.
3. <u>Experiential Learning Exercise</u>: Engage in critical thinking activities to better understand a vital issue. Examples of activities include debate and presentations.
4. <u>Reflection and Synthesis</u>: Record in your journal your reflections on the experience and in what ways your perspectives changed on the issue. Journal entries can be used as a "springboard" for a persuasive essay that addresses the target question of the vital issue. Your teacher may elicit your responses to the exercise.
5. <u>Evaluation</u>:
   a. Formal Assessment—Evaluate your essay with your teacher using an essay criterion reference sheet or rubric.
   b. Informal Assessment—Compare what you saw (your presumptions) with what you did not see (what you learned).

About the Learning Activities

(*Refer to ELA Template for more detail on page vii*)

The Activity Process
Learning activities always follow the same process:

Activities	Assessment
Free writing ⟶	Culturally-based presumptions
Information Gap Writing ⟶	New knowledge
Hands-On Activities: ⟶ 1. Bastiat Activity 2. Real-World Activity	Experiential learning
Journal Writing ⟶	Reflection and synthesis
Evaluation Notes ⟶	Evaluation

The first activity is a free writing activity to discover your culturally-based presumptions about the topic under discussion.

The second activity is an information gap activity. Here you gain new knowledge and then compare your presumptions with the new knowledge.

The third activity is the hands-on activity which is the "experiential learning" phase of ELA. You will a) engage in the reading of Bastiat's *What Is Seen and What Is Not Seen* and use your systems thinking tools to understand free market mechanisms as Bastiat describes them, and b) apply your systems thinking tools to real-world economic situations, such as the financial crisis of 2008-2009. IMPORTANT: For "What Is NOT Seen" CLDs in the Appendix, dotted lines are used to illustrate "what is not seen."

The fourth activity is journal writing. This helps you to record your reactions to the learning.

The fifth and final activity is the evaluation notes. In evaluation notes you compare "what you saw" (your presumptions) with "what you did not see" (what you learned). Your teacher might ask for a formal essay using a writing rubric to evaluate your learning. Or, you may be asked to do an informal assessment comparing what you saw (your presumptions) with what you did not see (what you learned).

Systemic Thinking Tools
Mastering the systemic thinking tools requires a lot of practice with real-world examples. That is why these activities have been designed to help you practice using them with real-life economic situations. Better said, many activities we do, or are affected by, every day are economic activities; and economic activities are systemic activities. So, before jumping into Bastiat's readings, we recommend you master the tools in *Systems Thinking Basics*.

Furthermore, the Appendix contains the "Learning Activity Key Points and Suggested Responses" for the "Bastiat Activity" so you can check your responses. However, please remember there is no one absolute way to describe and diagram a system. The activities and suggested responses are supposed to help you imagine how an economic system operates as well as serve as a starting point for you to cognitize economic systems.

Acknowledgments

The author and publisher sincerely thank the Foundation for Economic Education (FEE) for allowing us to re-print Frédéric Bastiat's *What Is Seen and What Is Not Seen*. The full downloadable version of Bastiat's work can be obtained from the FEE website at
http://fee.org/doc/selected_essays_on_politcal_economy/.

In addition, we wish to thank Pegasus Communications for its support by allowing us to quote and summarize material from *Systems Thinking Basics*.

The author also wishes to acknowledge the Harvard Graduate School of Education's Project Zero (PZ) Summer Institute for providing the intellectual stimulation and guidance in developing his version of an ELA. It was due to conversations with Howard Gardner, Steven Seidel, Tina Blythe, and PZ summer institute colleagues that he was able to conceptualize his version of an ELA cycle. He is grateful for their teaching and support over the years, and he hopes that this activity book will serve as a demonstration of the confluences of thought with them and the systems thinking community with which he is proud to belong.

ELA Template

Step 1

Free Writing

<u>Culturally-based presumptions</u>
Write what you think happens in the economy when….

<u>1st. Mind Map</u>: Map out your ideas using the systems thinking techniques of Behavior Over Time (BOT) graphs and Causal Loop Diagrams (CLDs).

<u>2nd. Map-to-Paper</u>: Write-out on a piece of paper in complete logical sentences in one paragraph or more your mind map. Ask yourself, "Does this make sense to me?" Then, ask someone to read what you wrote and compare your Mind Map with your Map-to-Paper.

> ## Step 2
>
> ## Information Gap Writing
>
> <u>New knowledge</u>
> Read …. Compare your presumptions with what is learned.

1st. <u>Read</u>: Read the topic which Bastiat discusses. Make notes of what you are reading.

2nd. <u>Compare</u>: Compare your presumptions with the new ideas from Bastiat. Ask yourself, "Are there any gaps between what I think and what Bastiat thinks?" Make a table like the one below. Fill in the blanks for each:

a.   Write your presumptions in the left box.
b.   Write what Bastiat thinks in the center box.
c.   Write the information gaps between you and Bastiat in the right box.

Presumptions	New Knowledge	Information Gaps

Experiential Learning Approach (ELA) Template

Step 3

Hands-On Activity 1

<u>Experiential Learning</u>
Draw a BOT graph and CLDs of Bastiat's description of "what is seen" and "what is not seen" in the economy when someone....

Hands-On Activity 2

<u>Experiential Learning</u>
Draw a BOT graph and CLDs of "what is seen" and "what is not seen" in the economy as a result of....

1st. <u>Do Hands-On Activity 1</u>: Learn with Bastiat by drawing BOT graphs and CLDs of his descriptions in the readings. Check your answers by referring to the Appendix.

2nd. <u>Do Hands-On Activity 2</u>: Apply what you have learned by drawing BOT graphs and CLDs for a real-world economic situation.

What Is Seen and What Is Not Seen: Fun Systems Thinking Activities with Frédéric Bastiat

---

Step 4

Journal Writing

<u>Reflection and Synthesis</u>
Record in a journal your reactions to the learning.

I learned a lot from this lesson. Before I thought that.... Now I learned that.....
_____
_____
_____
_____
_____
_____
_____

Experiential Learning Approach (ELA) Template

Step 5

Evaluation Notes

<u>Evaluation</u>

Compare "what you saw" (your presumptions) with "what you did not see" (what you learned).

What I saw	What I did not see
1. I first saw….. .	1. But what I did not see was…

Systems Thinking Basics
Review

Systems Thinking Basics Review*

What is a system?

Virginia Anderson and Lauren Keller Johnson in *Systems Thinking Basics* define a system as "a group of interacting, interrelated, or interdependent components that form a complex unified whole." To put it another way, a "heap" is the simple sum of the parts of an entity, such as a car engine. If we dismantle a car engine, we can say that 1+1=2. But, when we put the car engine together and make it an interacting, interrelated part of an automobile, then we call it a system, we can say that 1+1=2 + Synergistic Relationship. The synergistic relationship is the car engine interacting with the other parts of the automobile, so it is more than just the sum of the engine's parts; it is the entire engine system in motion.

The key points for understanding a system are what we can call (I-CUP):

1. Interacting, Interrelated, Interdependent (3I's)
2. Complex
3. Unified
4. Purposeful

Furthermore, the defining characteristics of systems are:

1. A system's parts must all be present for the system to carry out its purpose optimally.
2. A system's parts must be arranged in a specific way for the system to carry out its purpose.
3. Systems have specific purposes within larger systems.
4. Systems maintain their stability through fluctuations and adjustments.
5. Systems have feedback.

Finally, systems are built on structures that make evident a system's existence. We cannot see an entire economic system, but we know it exists because its structures are evident to us. The structures that make systems include: events, patterns, systemic structure, mental models, and vision.

Figure 1. Systems In Context

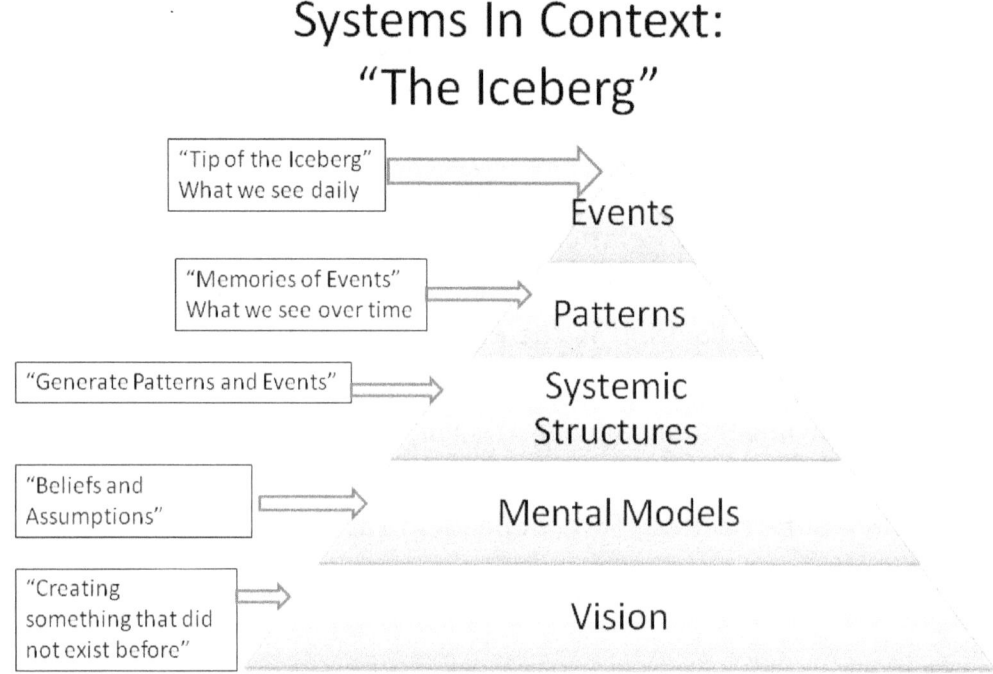

Referring to Figure 1, we can see that a system is built like an iceberg. At the tip of the iceberg are events. Events are what we actually see on a daily basis. For example, in reference to Figure 2, when the financial crisis of 2008-2009 happened, we read it in the daily news headlines. On one day we read that people were defaulting on their home loans. On another day we read that the sub-prime loan securities became worthless. On another day we read that the housing market crashed. On another day we read that the investment banks went bankrupt. Then, on another day we read that people were losing their jobs. Finally we read that we were in a recession and the vicious cycle has continued ever since, even up to the date of writing this book. This is what we read and continue to read in the news headlines on a daily basis.

Figure 2. Events: The Financial Crisis News Headlines Vicious Cycle

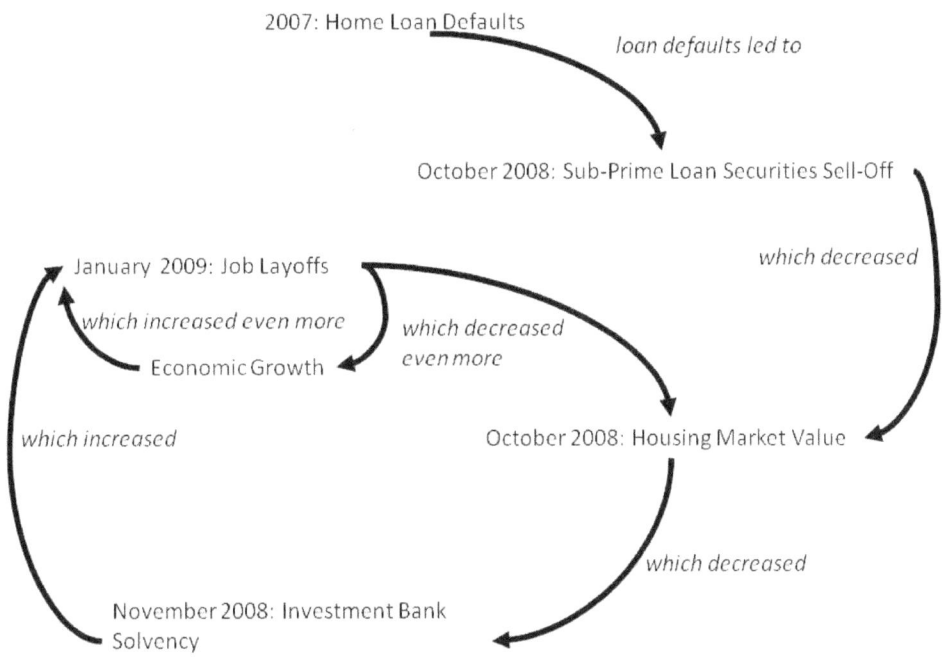

We can see that it was over the course of time that these news headlines showed the "patterns" of the financial crisis. Anyone who was a news commentator at this time gave his or her two bits on describing these patterns. It was only later when Congress decided to have hearings did former Federal Reserve Bank Chairman, Alan Greenspan, make the "systemic structures" and "mental models" evident to the public. Systemic structures generate patterns and events, and for the financial crisis of 2008-2009 these structures included the "financial system" as Mr. Greenspan had best described it. These structures, as Mr. Greenspan himself acknowledged in the hearings, were built upon mental models, that is, "beliefs and assumptions" about free market activities. Unfortunately, as Mr. Greenspan testified, his mental models were not completely accurate. This does not mean that his "vision" of a free market economy was not accurate. It only means that some of his beliefs and assumptions about human action in a free market were incorrect. It is only the effects of these beliefs and assumptions that we see; we do not see clearly, however, the beliefs and assumptions themselves. Therefore, understanding a system in its context will allow you to better understand the system, and this is the purpose of this activity book (refer to Figure 3).

Figure 3. Re-Cap of a System in Context

Re-Cap

Systems in Context	Action Mode	Time Orientation	Way of Perceiving	Questions You Would Ask
Events	React	Present	Witness Event	"What's the fastest way to react to this event now?"
Patterns	Adapt		Measure or Track Patterns of Events	"What kinds of trends or patterns of events seem to be recurring?"
Structure	Create Change		Causal Loop Diagrams and Other Systems Thinking Tools	"What structures are in place that are causing these patterns?"
Mental Models	Believe		Statement of "I Believe"	"What is the purpose of the system?"
Vision	Imagine	Future	Statement of "Should Be"	"What should be the system?"

What is systems thinking?

Systems thinking is a way of thinking about the interconnections between the parts of a system and their synthesis into a unified view of the whole system. Virginia Anderson and Lauren Johnson characterize systems thinking into the following principles:

1. Thinking of the "big picture";
2. Balancing short-term and long-term perspectives;
3. Recognizing the dynamic, complex, and interdependent nature of systems;
4. Taking into account both measurable and non-measurable factors;

5. Remembering that we are all part of the systems in which we function, and that we each influence those systems even as we are being influenced by them.

Therefore, when we use the language of systems thinking, we should be talking in the following ways:

Talk about...
- Wholes
- Interconnections
- How we influence systems

Talk in...
- Circular language
- Precise set of rules that reduce ambiguities and miscommunications

Talk with...
- Visual tools, such as behavior over time graphs and causal loop diagrams
- Mental models to translate our perceptions into explicit pictures

What is a Behavior Over Time (BOT) Graph?

A BOT graph is basically the graphing of systemic structural variables over time. To do this, we need to follow several steps:

1. Formulate the problem
2. Identify the key variables of the problem (the main actors)
3. Graph the behaviors of these variables over time

Let us return to our financial crisis example to demonstrate this. The key variables for this crisis may include:

- The number of home loan re-payments
- The number of sub-prime loan security trades
- The number of home sales
- The amount of investment bank profits
- The number of employed workers
- The amount of government intervention into the economy

Also, there are several important points to be made when naming our variables. First, use nouns or noun phrases, *not* verbs or verb phrases. Second, use phrases such as "the level of," "the amount of," "the number of," and "the size of". Third, use a neutral or positive term, such as "profits," this way you will be able to describe the way in which the variable changes, such as "increases," "decreases," "improves," "worsens." Finally, remember that variables can be either concrete things, such as houses, or intangibles, such as consumer satisfaction.

Figure 4. BOT Graph of the 2008-2009 US Financial Crisis

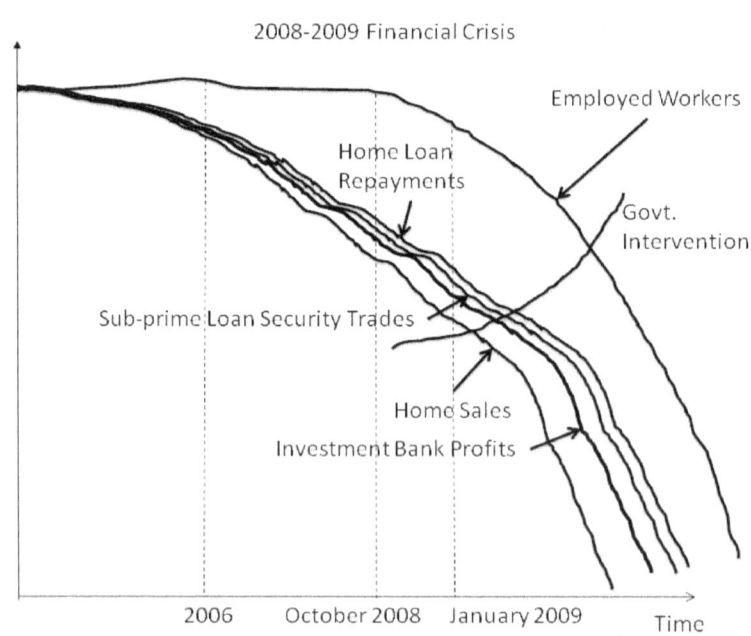

In our example we see all the key variables. Notice that all but one of the variables decline. Also notice that there is a lag between unemployment and October 2008 when the financial crisis actually hit the news. Ever since 2006 financial experts were aware of a housing bubble as well as the sub-prime loan securities (derivatives) being traded on the stock exchange and that an increase in home loan defaults would cause the value of the derivatives to decrease; thus making them "toxic assets." So, the time-span between home loan repayments and sub-prime loan security trades are very near and both have a positive correlation. Home sales also have a positive correlation, but lag ahead loan defaults and security trades since home sales are dependent upon new home buyers.

Another aspect of our BOT graph is the day of the crash. Since 2006 "market insiders" knew that the derivatives were losing value as home loans that were packaged into these derivates defaulted. This means that the profits of the financial houses were declining, but were never actually recorded as loses. It is in October 2008 when we see a sharp decline in the profits of the financial houses, even some of them going bust, and then a government intervention plan or bailout soon afterwards, which is referred to as TARP (Troubled Assets Relief Program).

What is a Causal Loop Diagram (CLD)?

A CLD is a drawn representation of the systemic structure under investigation. It allows you to a) explore the dynamic interrelationships among variables in the structure, b) see how parts of the system are separated by location and/or time, and c) hypothesize about possible solutions to the systemic problem and then test them. In sum, CLDs contain the following components:

- One or more feedback loops that are reinforcing or balancing processes
- Cause-and-effect relationships among the system variables
- Delays

If we consider the financial crisis example again, we can draw a simple CLD to explain how it works. As with any CLD, you need to walk yourself through the loop to make sure you have drawn it correctly. First, we identify our variables: economic activity, employment, disposable income, and government intervention. Next, we plot the variables and their relationships, as shown in Figure 5.

Figure 5. CLD Reinforcing Loop

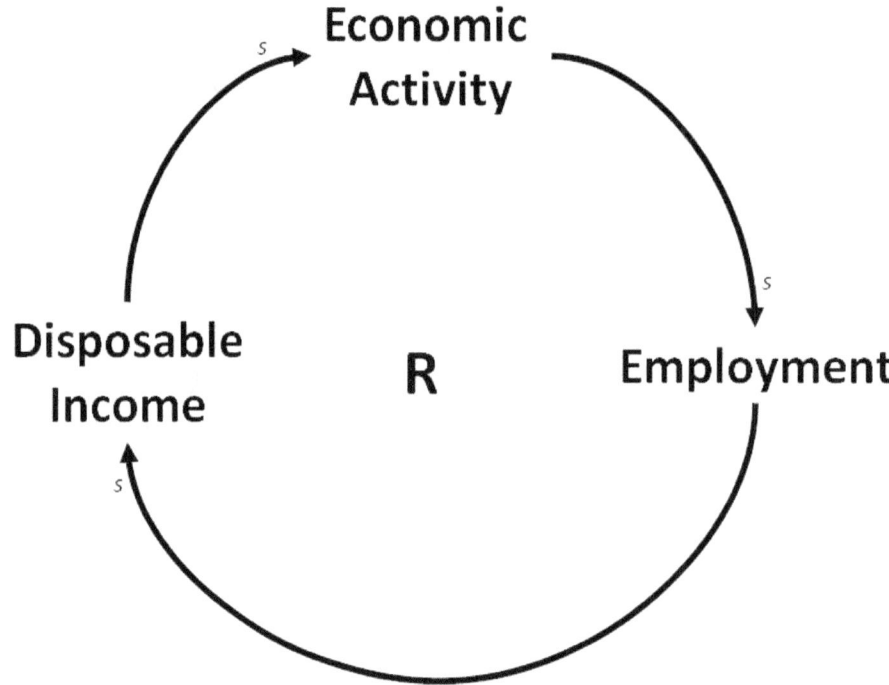

Walk-through the Loop
R-Loop
First, the culminating financial problems in the economy have led to a decline in economic activity (↓). This decline in economic activity causes a decline in employment (↓). Therefore, we put an "s" next to the arrow to show that the actor causes the action recipient to move in the same direction, which is "down" in this case. This decline in employment causes a decline in disposable income (↓), and we put an "s" next to this arrow as well. Finally, to close the loop, a decline in disposable income causes a further decline in economic activity because either

people have lost their jobs and have no disposable income or those who do have jobs are worried about the future and do not spend as much money as before, and we put an "s" next to this arrow, too.

As you can see, all the arrows move in the same direction. This loop is an illustration of a reinforcing loop, so we put an "R" in the center of the loop. A reinforcing loop creates rapid growth or collapse by driving change in one direction with increasing change in the same direction each time you go around the loop. In the case of the financial crisis, a decline in economic activity has caused a decline in employment which has caused a decline in disposable income which has caused a further decline in economic activity.

B-Loop
In order to maintain or increase economic activity as a result of the financial crisis, several government interventions have occurred. Under the Bush Administration, Congress implemented the Troubled Assets Relief Program (TARP). Then, under the Obama Administration, Congress extended unemployment benefits as well as created a "jobs" program.

We call these government interventions balancing actions because they are goal seeking. The goal is to restore, maintain, and/or increase economic activity. Therefore, the relationship between economic activity and government intervention is an inverse relationship. If economic activity declines (↓), then government intervention increases (↑), so we place an "o" next to the arrow to show the movement in the "opposite" direction. However, as is illustrated in Figure 6, the interventions are delayed actions. Though the government intervention increases employment, "s" arrow, it does not happen quickly. After all, whenever Congress passes an emergency appropriations bill, it takes time for the money to actually circulate through the economy. So, we write the word "delay" across the arrow.

Figure 6. CLD Balancing Loop

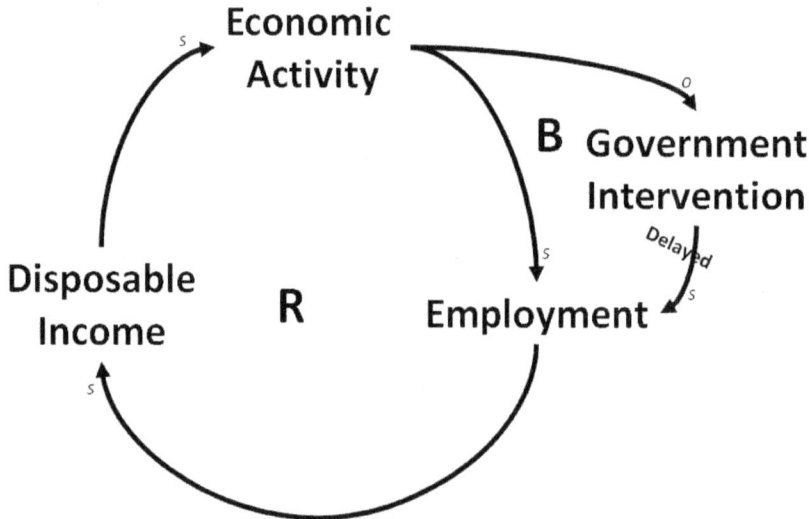

One final note about drawing CLDs, if the loop is a balancing loop, it will have an odd number of "o's". If it is a reinforcing loop, it will have an even number of "o's" or no "o's".

1. Balancing Loop = Odd number of "o's"
2. Reinforcing Loop = Even number of "o's" or No "o's"

However, you should always double-check your work by walking yourself through the loop.

This concludes our review of the basics of systems thinking. If you have forgotten some of the concepts and need more practice, please refer to *Systems Thinking Basics* and practice the exercises. However, if you feel comfortable with the basics, then you are ready to move on to learning free market economics with Bastiat.

---

* This is a summary of *Systems Thinking Basics* and should be referred to for complete understanding and practice of the systems thinking concepts and tools used in this activity book.

Units

Unit 1: Introduction and The Broken Window

Step 1

Free Writing

<u>Culturally-based presumptions</u>
Write what you think happens in the economy when someone throws a rock through someone's window.

Unit 1: The Broken Window

Step 2

Information Gap Writing

<u>New knowledge</u>
Read the "Introduction" and "The Broken Window." Compare your presumptions with what is learned.

Presumptions	New Knowledge	Information Gaps

What Is Seen and What is Not Seen[1]

Introduction

In the economic sphere an act, a habit, an institution, a law produces not only one effect, but a series of effects. Of these effects, the first alone is immediate; it appears simultaneously with its cause; *it is seen*. The other effects emerge only subsequently; *they are not seen;* we are fortunate if we *foresee* them.

There is only one difference between a bad economist and a good one: the bad economist confines himself to the *visible* effect; the good economist takes into account both the effect that can be seen and those effects that must be *foreseen*.

Yet this difference is tremendous; for it almost always happens that when the immediate consequence is favorable, the later consequences are disastrous, and vice versa. Whence it follows that the bad economist pursues a small present good that will be followed by a great evil to come, while the good economist pursues a great good to come, at the risk of a small present evil.

The same thing, of course, is true of health and morals. Often, the sweeter the first fruit of a habit, the more bitter are its later fruits: for example, debauchery, sloth, prodigality. When a man is impressed by the effect *that is seen* and has not yet learned to discern the effects *that are not seen*, he indulges in deplorable habits, not only through natural inclination, but deliberately.

This explains man's necessarily painful evolution. Ignorance surrounds him at his cradle; therefore, he regulates his acts according to their first consequences, the only ones that, in his infancy, he can see. It is only after a long time that he learns to take account of the others[2]. Two very different masters teach him this lesson: experience and foresight. Experience teaches efficaciously but brutally. It instructs us in all the effects of an act by making us feel them, and we cannot fail to learn eventually, from having been burned ourselves, that fire burns. I should prefer, in so far as possible, to replace this rude teacher with one more gentle: foresight. For that reason I shall investigate the consequences of several economic phenomena, contrasting those *that are seen* with those *that are not seen*.

The Broken Window

Have you ever been witness to the fury of that solid citizen, James Goodfellow[*], when his incorrigible son has happened to break a pane of glass? If you have been present at this spectacle, certainly you must also have observed that the onlookers, even if there are as many as thirty of them, seem with one accord to offer the unfortunate owner the selfsame consolation: "It's an ill wind that blows nobody some good. Such accidents keep industry going. Everybody has to make a living. What would become of the glaziers if no one ever broke a window?"

Now, this formula of condolence contains a whole theory that it is a good idea for us to expose, *flagrante delicto*, in this very simple case, since it is exactly the same as that which, unfortunately, underlies most of our economic institutions.

Suppose that it will cost six francs to repair the damage. If you mean that the accident gives six francs' worth of encouragement to the aforesaid industry, I agree. I do not contest it in any way; your reasoning is correct. The glazier will come, do his job, receive six francs, congratulate himself, and bless in his heart the careless child. *That is what is seen.*

But if, by way of deduction, you conclude, as happens only too often, that it is good to break windows, that it helps to circulate money, that it results in encouraging industry in general, I am obliged to cry out: That will never do! Your theory stops at *what is seen.* It does not take account of *what is not seen.*

It is not seen that, since our citizen has spent six francs for one thing, he will not be able to spend them for another. *It is not seen* that if he had not had a windowpane to replace, he would have replaced, for example, his worn-out shoes or added another book to his library. In brief, he would have put his six francs to some use or other for which he will not now have them.

Let us next consider industry *in general.* The window having been broken, the glass industry gets six francs' worth of encouragement; *that is what is seen.*

---

[*] [In French, *Jacques Bonhomme*, used like "John Bull" in English to represent the practical, responsible, unassuming average man.—Translator.]

If the window had not been broken, the shoe industry (or some other) would have received six francs' worth of encouragement; *that is what is not seen.*

And if we were to take into consideration *what is not seen*, because it is a negative factor, as well as *what is seen*, because it is a positive factor, we should understand that there is no benefit to industry *in general* or to *national employment* as a whole, whether windows are broken or not broken.

Now let us consider James Goodfellow.

On the first hypothesis, that of the broken window, he spends six francs and has, neither more nor less than before, the enjoyment of one window.

On the second, that in which the accident did not happen, he would have spent six francs for new shoes and would have had the enjoyment of a pair of shoes as well as of a window.

Now, if James Goodfellow is part of society, we must conclude that society, considering its labors and its enjoyments, has lost the value of the broken window.

From which, by generalizing, we arrive at this unexpected conclusion: "Society loses the value of objects unnecessarily destroyed," and at this aphorism, which will make the hair of the protectionists stand on end: "To break, to destroy, to dissipate is not to encourage national employment," or more briefly: "Destruction is not profitable."

What will the *Moniteur industriel*[†] say to this, or the disciples of the estimable M. de Saint-Chamans[‡], who has calculated with such precision what industry would gain from the burning of Paris, because of the houses that would have to be rebuilt?

[†] [Newspaper of the Committee for the Defense of Domestic Industry, a protectionist organization.—Translator.]

[‡] [Auguste, Vicomte de Saint-Chamans (1777–1861), Deputy and Councillor of State under the Restoration, protectionist and upholder of the balance of trade. His celebrated stand on the "obstacle" here quoted by Bastiat comes from his *Nouvel essai sur la richesse des nations,* 1824. This work was later (1852) incorporated in his *Traité d'économie politique.*—Translator.]

I am sorry to upset his ingenious calculations, especially since their spirit has passed into our legislation. But I beg him to begin them again, entering *what is not seen* in the ledger beside *what is seen*.

The reader must apply himself to observe that there are not only two people, but three, in the little drama that I have presented. The one, James Goodfellow, represents the consumer, reduced by destruction to one enjoyment instead of two. The other, under the figure of the glazier, shows us the producer whose industry the accident encourages. The third is the shoemaker (or any other manufacturer) whose industry is correspondingly discouraged by the same cause. It is this third person who is always in the shadow, and who, personifying *what is not seen*, is an essential element of the problem. It is he who makes us understand how absurd it is to see a profit in destruction. It is he who will soon teach us that it is equally absurd to see a profit in trade restriction, which is, after all, nothing more nor less than partial destruction. So, if you get to the bottom of all the arguments advanced in favor of restrictionist measures, you will find only a paraphrase of that common cliché: "*What would become of the glaziers if no one ever broke any windows?*"

---

[1] [This pamphlet, published in July, 1850, is the last that Bastiat wrote. It had been promised to the public for more than a year. Its publication had been delayed because the author had lost the manuscript when he moved his household from the rue de Choiseul to the rue d'Algen. After a long and fruitless search, he decided to rewrite his work entirely, and chose as the principal basis of his demonstrations some speeches recently delivered in the National Assembly. When this task was finished, he reproached himself with having been too serious, threw the second manuscript into the fire, and wrote the one which we reprint.—Editor.]

[2] [See chap. 10 of *Economic Harmonies*.—Editor.]

Step 3

Hands-On Activity 1

Experiential Learning

Draw two BOT graphs, one for window replacement purchase and one for shoe purchase. Then, draw CLDs of Bastiat's description of "what is seen" and "what is not seen" in the economy for both purchases.

Hands-On Activity 2

Experiential Learning

Draw BOT graphs and CLDs of "what is seen" and "what is not seen" in the economy as a result of the British Petroleum oil disaster in the Gulf of Mexico.

Activity 1 BOT: The Broken Window

Window Replacement Purchase	Shoe Purchase

Unit 1: The Broken Window

Activity 1 CLD: Window *What Is Seen*	*What Is NOT Seen*

Activity 1 CLD: Shoes *What Is Seen*	*What Is NOT Seen*

Activity 2 BOT	
What Is Seen	*What Is NOT Seen*

Activity 2 CLD	
What Is Seen	*What Is NOT Seen*

Unit 1: The Broken Window

Step 4

Journal Writing

<u>Reflection and Synthesis</u>
Record in a journal your reactions to the learning.

Step 5

Evaluation Notes

<u>Evaluation</u>
Compare "what you saw" (your presumptions) with "what you did not see" (what you learned).

What I saw	What I did not see
1. I first saw..... .	1. But what I did not see was…

Unit 2: The Demobilization

Step 1

Free Writing

<u>Culturally-based presumptions</u>
Write what you think happens in the economy when a government mobilizes troops for war.

_____
_____
_____
_____
_____
_____
_____
_____
_____
_____

Unit 2: The Demobilization

Step 2

Information Gap Writing

<u>New knowledge</u>
Read "The Demobilization." Compare your presumptions with what is learned.

Presumptions	New Knowledge	Information Gaps

23

The Demobilization

A nation is in the same case as a man. When a man wishes to give himself a satisfaction, he has to see whether it is worth what it costs. For a nation, security is the greatest of blessings. If, to acquire it, a hundred thousand men must be mobilized, and a hundred million francs spent, I have nothing to say. It is an enjoyment bought at the price of a sacrifice.

Let there be no misunderstanding, then, about the point I wish to make in what I have to say on this subject.

A legislator proposes to discharge a hundred thousand men, which will relieve the taxpayers of a hundred million francs in taxes.

Suppose we confine ourselves to replying to him: "These one hundred thousand men and these one hundred million francs are indispensable to our national security. It is a sacrifice; but without this sacrifice France would be torn by internal factions or invaded from without." I have no objection here to this argument, which may be true or false as the case may be, but which theoretically does not constitute any economic heresy. The heresy begins when the sacrifice itself is represented as an advantage, because it brings profit to someone.

Now, if I am not mistaken, no sooner will the author of the proposal have descended from the platform, than an orator will rush up and say:

"Discharge a hundred thousand men! What are you thinking of? What will become of them? What will they live on? On their earnings? But do you not know that there is unemployment everywhere? That all occupations are oversupplied? Do you wish to throw them on the market to increase the competition and to depress wage rates? Just at the moment when it is difficult to earn a meager living, is it not fortunate that the state is giving bread to a hundred thousand individuals? Consider further that the army consumes wine, clothes, and weapons, that it thus spreads business to the factories and the garrison towns, and that it is nothing less than a godsend to its innumerable suppliers. Do you not tremble at the idea of bringing this immense industrial activity to an end?"

This speech, we see, concludes in favor of maintaining a hundred thousand soldiers, not because of the nation's need for the services rendered by the army, but for economic reasons. It is these considerations alone that I propose to refute.

A hundred thousand men, costing the taxpayers a hundred million francs, live as well and provide as good a living for their suppliers as a hundred million francs will allow: *that is what is seen.*

But a hundred million francs, coming from the pockets of the taxpayers, ceases to provide a living for these taxpayers and *their* suppliers, to the extent of a hundred million francs: *that is what is not seen.* Calculate, figure, and tell me where there is any profit for the mass of the people.

I will, for my part, tell you where the *loss* is, and to simplify things, instead of speaking of a hundred thousand men and a hundred million francs, let us talk about one man and a thousand francs.

Here we are in the village of A. The recruiters make the rounds and muster one man. The tax collectors make their rounds also and raise a thousand francs. The man and the sum are transported to Metz, the one destined to keep the other alive for a year without doing anything. If you look only at Metz, yes, you are right a hundred times; the procedure is very advantageous. But if you turn your eyes to the village of A, you will judge otherwise, for, unless you are blind, you will see that this village has lost a laborer and the thousand francs that would remunerate his labor, and the business which, through the spending of these thousand francs, he would spread about him.

At first glance it seems as if the loss is compensated. What took place at the village now takes place at Metz, and that is all there is to it. But here is where the loss is. In the village a man dug and labored: he was a worker; at Metz he goes through "Right dress!" and "Left dress!": he is a soldier. The money involved and its circulation are the same in both cases: but in one there were three hundred days of productive labor; in the other there are three hundreds days of unproductive labor, on the supposition, of course, that a part of the army is not indispensable to public security.

Now comes demobilization. You point out to me a surplus of a hundred thousand workers, intensified competition and the pressure that it exerts on wage rates. That is what you see.

But here is what you do not see. You do not see that to send home a hundred thousand soldiers is not to do away with a hundred million francs, but to return that money to the taxpayers. You do not see that to throw a hundred thousand workers on the market in this way is to throw in at the same time the hundred million francs destined to pay for their labor; that, as a consequence, the same measure that increases the *supply* of workers also increases the *demand;* from which it follows that your lowering of wages is illusory. You do not see that before, as well as after, the demobilization there are a hundred million francs corresponding to the hundred thousand men; that the whole difference consists in this: that before, the country gives the hundred million francs to the hundred thousand men for doing nothing; afterwards, it gives them the money for working. Finally, you do not see that when a taxpayer gives his money, whether to a soldier in exchange for nothing or to a worker in exchange for something, all the more remote consequences of the circulation of this money are the same in both cases: only, in the second case the taxpayer receives something; in the first he receives nothing. Result: a dead loss for the nation.

The sophism that I am attacking here cannot withstand the test of extended application, which is the touchstone of all theoretical principles. If, all things considered, there is a *national profit* in increasing the size of the army, why not call the whole male population of the country to the colors?

Unit 2: The Demobilization

Step 3

Hands-On Activity 1

<u>Experiential Learning</u>
Draw two BOT graphs, one for mobilization and one for demobilization. Then draw one CLD of Bastiat's description of "what is seen" and "what is not seen" in the economy for mobilization and demobilization of a hundred thousand men to perform military training which will cost the taxpayer a hundred million francs for mobilization.

Hands-On Activity 2

<u>Experiential Learning</u>
Find a news article about the Iraq or Afghanistan wars and draw BOT graphs and CLDs of "what is seen" and "what is not seen" in the economy as a result of a state mobilizing its national guard for either war.

Activity 1 BOT: The Demobilization

Mobilization	*Demobilization*

Activity 1 CLD: Mobilization and Demobilization

Activity 2 BOT

Unit 2: The Demobilization

Activity 2 CLD

Step 4

Journal Writing

Reflection and Synthesis
Record in a journal your reactions to the learning.

Step 5

Evaluation Notes

<u>Evaluation</u>
Compare "what you saw" (your presumptions) with "what you did not see" (what you learned).

What I saw	What I did not see
1. I first saw..... .	1. But what I did not see was...

Unit 3: Taxes

> ## Step 1
>
> ## Free Writing
>
> <u>Culturally-based presumptions</u>
> Write what you think happens in the economy when a government imposes taxes.

Step 2

Information Gap Writing

<u>New knowledge</u>
Read "Taxes." Compare your presumptions with what is learned.

Presumptions	New Knowledge	Information Gaps

Taxes

Have you ever heard anyone say: "Taxes are the best investment; they are a life-giving dew. See how many families they keep alive, and follow in imagination their indirect effects on industry; they are infinite, as extensive as life itself."

To combat this doctrine, I am obliged to repeat the preceding refutation. Political economy knows very well that its arguments are not diverting enough for anyone to say about them: *Repetita placent;* repetition pleases. So, like Basile[*], political economy has "arranged" the proverb for its own use, quite convinced that, from its mouth, *Repetita docent;* repetition teaches.

The advantages that government officials enjoy in drawing their salaries are *what is seen*. The benefits that result for their suppliers are also *what is seen*. They are right under your nose.

But the disadvantage that the taxpayers try to free themselves from is *what is not seen*, and the distress that results from it for the merchants who supply them is *something further that is not seen*, although it should stand out plainly enough to be seen intellectually.

When a government official spends on his own behalf one hundred sous more, this implies that a taxpayer spends on his own behalf one hundred sous the less. But the spending of the government official is *seen*, because it is done; while that of the taxpayer *is not seen*, because—alas!—he is prevented from doing it.

You compare the nation to a parched piece of land and the tax to a life-giving rain. So be it. But you should also ask yourself where this rain comes from, and whether it is not precisely the tax that draws the moisture from the soil and dries it up.

You should ask yourself further whether the soil receives more of this precious water from the rain than it loses by the evaporation?

What is quite certain is that, when James Goodfellow counts out a hundred sous to the tax collector, he receives nothing in return. When, then, a government official, in spending these

---

[*] [In Act II of *The Barber of Seville*, Basile, the musician, says: "I have arranged several proverbs with variations."—Translator.]

hundred sous, returns them to James Goodfellow, it is for an equivalent value in wheat or in labor. The final result is a loss of five francs for James Goodfellow.

It is quite true that often, nearly always if you will, the government official renders an equivalent service to James Goodfellow. In this case there is no loss on either side; there is only an exchange. Therefore, my argument is not in any way concerned with useful functions. I say this: If you wish to create a government office, prove its usefulness. Demonstrate that to James Goodfellow it is worth the equivalent of what it costs him by virtue of the services it renders him. But apart from this intrinsic utility, do not cite, as an argument in favor of opening the new bureau, the advantage that it constitutes for the bureaucrat, his family, and those who supply his needs; do not allege that it encourages employment.

When James Goodfellow gives a hundred sous to a government official for a really useful service, this is exactly the same as when he gives a hundred sous to a shoemaker for a pair of shoes. It's a case of give-and-take, and the score is even. But when James Goodfellow hands over a hundred sous to a government official to receive no service for it or even to be subjected to inconveniences, it is as if he were to give his money to a thief. It serves no purpose to say that the official will spend these hundred sous for the great profit of our *national industry;* the more the thief can do with them, the more James Goodfellow could have done with them if he had not met on his way either the extralegal or the legal parasite.

Let us accustom ourselves, then, not to judge things solely by *what is seen,* but rather by *what is not seen.*

Last year I was on the Finance Committee, for in the Constituent Assembly the members of the opposition were not systematically excluded from all committees. In this the framers of the Constitution acted wisely. We have heard M. Thiers[†] say: "I have spent my life fighting men of the legitimist party and of the clerical party. Since, in the face of a common danger, I have come to know them and we have had heart-to-heart talks, I see that they are not the monsters I had imagined."

[†] [Adolphe Thiers (1797–1877), French statesman and distinguished historian. In his long political career he was Deputy and Prime Minister (1836 and 1840), and, as a final tribute, was elected President of the Third Republic in 1871.—Translator.]

Unit 3: Taxes

Yes, enmities become exaggerated and hatreds are intensified between parties that do not mingle; and if the majority would allow a few members of the minority to penetrate into the circles of the committees, perhaps it would be recognized on both sides that their ideas are not so far apart, and above all that their intentions are not so perverse, as supposed.

However that may be, last year I was on the Finance Committee. Each time that one of our colleagues spoke of fixing at a moderate figure the salaries of the President of the Republic, of cabinet ministers, and of ambassadors, he would be told:

"For the good of the service, we must surround certain offices with an aura of prestige and dignity. That is the way to attract to them men of merit. Innumerable unfortunate people turn to the President of the Republic, and he would be in a painful position if he were always forced to refuse them help. A certain amount of ostentation in the ministerial and diplomatic salons is part of the machinery of constitutional governments, etc., etc."

Whether or not such arguments can be controverted, they certainly deserve serious scrutiny. They are based on the public interest, rightly or wrongly estimated; and, personally, I can make more of a case for them than many of our Catos, moved by a narrow spirit of [miserliness] or jealousy.

But what shocks my economist's conscience, what makes me blush for the intellectual renown of my country, is when they go on from these arguments (as they never fail to do) to this absurd banality (always favorably received):

"Besides, the luxury of high officials of the government encourages the arts, industry, and employment. The Chief of State and his ministers cannot give banquets and parties without infusing life into all the veins of the body politic. To reduce their salaries would be to starve industry in Paris and, at the same time, throughout the nation."

For heaven's sake, gentlemen, at least respect arithmetic, and do not come before the National Assembly of France and say, for fear that, to its shame, it will not support you, that an addition gives a different sum depending upon whether it is added from top to bottom or from bottom to top.

Well, then, suppose I arrange to have a navvy dig me a ditch in my field for the sum of a hundred sous. Just as I conclude this agreement, the tax collector takes my hundred sous from me and has them passed on to the Minister of the Interior. My contract is broken, but the Minister will add another dish at his dinner. On what basis do you dare to affirm that this official expenditure is an addition to the national industry? Do you not see that it is only a simple *transfer* of consumption and of labor? A cabinet minister has his table more lavishly set, it is true; but a farmer has his field less well drained, and this is just as true. A Parisian caterer has gained a hundred sous, I grant you; but grant me that a provincial ditchdigger has lost five francs. All that one can say is that the official dish and the satisfied caterer are *what is seen;* the swampy field and the excavator out of work are *what is not seen.*

Good Lord! What a lot of trouble to prove in political economy that two and two make four; and if you succeed in doing so, people cry, "It is so clear that it is boring." Then they vote as if you had never proved anything at all.

Step 3

Hands-On Activity 1

Experiential Learning

Draw two BOT graphs and one CLD of Bastiat's description of "what is seen" and "what is not seen" in the economy when a government imposes taxes.

Hands-On Activity 2

Experiential Learning

Find a news article about your local, state, or national government imposing a tax and draw BOT graphs and CLDs of "what is seen" and "what is not seen" in the economy as a result of the new tax.

Activity 1 BOT: Taxes What Is Seen	What Is NOT Seen

Activity 1 CLD

Activity 2 BOT

Unit 3: Taxes

Activity 2 CLD

Step 4

Journal Writing

<u>Reflection and Synthesis</u>
Record in a journal your reactions to the learning.

Step 5

Evaluation Notes

<u>Evaluation</u>
Compare "what you saw" (your presumptions) with "what you did not see" (what you learned).

What I saw	What I did not see
1. I first saw..... .	1. But what I did not see was…

Unit 4: Theaters and Fine Arts

> ## Step 1
>
> ## Free Writing
>
> Culturally-based presumptions
> Write what you think happens in the economy when taxes subsidize theaters and fine arts.

Step 2

Information Gap Writing

<u>New knowledge</u>
Read "Theaters and Fine Arts." Compare your presumptions with what is learned.

Presumptions	New Knowledge	Information Gaps

Theaters and Fine Arts

Should the state subsidize the arts?

There is certainly a great deal to say on this subject pro and con.

In favor of the system of subsidies, one can say that the arts broaden, elevate, and poetize the soul of a nation; that they draw it away from material preoccupations, giving it a feeling for the beautiful, and thus react favorably on its manners, its customs, its morals, and even on its industry. One can ask where music would be in France without the Théâtre-Italien and the Conservatory; dramatic art without the Théâtre-Français; painting and sculpture without our collections and our museums. One can go further and ask whether, without the centralization and consequently the subsidizing of the fine arts, there would have developed that exquisite taste which is the noble endowment of French labor and sends its products out over the whole world. In the presence of such results would it not be the height of imprudence to renounce this moderate assessment on all the citizens, which, in the last analysis, is what has achieved for them their pre-eminence and their glory in the eyes of Europe?

To these reasons and many others, whose power I do not contest, one can oppose many no less cogent. There is, first of all, one could say, a question of distributive justice. Do the rights of the legislator go so far as to allow him to dip into the wages of the artisan in order to supplement the profits of the artist? M. de Lamartine* said: "If you take away the subsidy of a theater, where are you going to stop on this path, and will you not be logically required to do away with your university faculties, your museums, your institutes, your libraries?" One could reply: If you wish to subsidize all that is good and useful, where are you going to stop on *that* path, and will you not logically be required to set up a civil list for agriculture, industry, commerce, welfare, and education? Furthermore, is it certain that subsidies favor the progress of the arts? It is a question that is far from being resolved, and we see with our own eyes that the theaters that prosper are those that live on their own profits. Finally, proceeding to higher considerations, one may observe that needs and desires give rise to one another and keep soaring into regions more and more rarefied[3] in proportion as the national wealth

---

* [Alphonse Marie Louis de Lamartine (1790–1869), one of the great poets of French romanticism and subsequently a distinguished statesman. First elected Deputy in 1834, he attained his greatest glory at the time of the Revolution of 1848, when he was a prime mover in the establishment of the Republic. By his eloquence he calmed the Paris mobs that threatened to destroy it and became the head of the provisional government. More an idealist and orator than a practical politician, however, he soon lost influence and retired to private life in 1851.—Translator.]

permits their satisfaction; that the government must not meddle in this process, since, whatever may be currently the amount of the national wealth, it cannot stimulate luxury industries by taxation without harming essential industries, thus reversing the natural advance of civilization. One may also point out that this artificial dislocation of wants, tastes, labor, and population places nations in a precarious and dangerous situation, leaving them without a solid base.

These are some of the reasons alleged by the adversaries of state intervention concerning the order in which citizens believe they should satisfy their needs and their desires, and thus direct their activity. I confess that I am one of those who think that the choice, the impulse, should come from below, not from above, from the citizens, not from the legislator; and the contrary doctrine seems to me to lead to the annihilation of liberty and of human dignity.

But, by an inference as false as it is unjust, do you know what the economists are now accused of? When we oppose subsidies, we are charged with opposing the very thing that it was proposed to subsidize and of being the enemies of all kinds of activity, because we want these activities to be voluntary and to seek their proper reward in themselves. Thus, if we ask that the state not intervene, by taxation, in religious matters, we are atheists. If we ask that the state not intervene, by taxation, in education, then we hate enlightenment. If we say that the state should not give, by taxation, an artificial value to land or to some branch of industry, then we are the enemies of property and of labor. If we think that the state should not subsidize artists, we are barbarians who judge the arts useless.

I protest with all my power against these inferences. Far from entertaining the absurd thought of abolishing religion, education, property, labor, and the arts when we ask the state to protect the free development of all these types of human activity without keeping them on the payroll at one another's expense, we believe, on the contrary, that all these vital forces of society should develop harmoniously under the influence of liberty and that none of them should become, as we see has happened today, a source of trouble, abuses, tyranny, and disorder.

Our adversaries believe that an activity that is neither subsidized nor regulated is abolished. We believe the contrary. Their faith is in the legislator, not in mankind. Ours is in mankind, not in the legislator.

Thus, M. de Lamartine said: "On the basis of this principle, we should have to *abolish* the public expositions that bring wealth and honor to this country."

I reply to M. de Lamartine: From your point of view, *not to subsidize* is *to abolish*, because, proceeding from the premise that nothing exists except by the will of the state, you conclude that nothing lives that taxes do not keep alive. But I turn against you the example that you have chosen, and I point out to you that the greatest, the noblest, of all expositions, the one based on the most liberal, the most universal conception, and I can even use the word "humanitarian," which is not here exaggerated, is the exposition now being prepared in London,† the only one in which no government meddles and which no tax supports.

Returning to the fine arts, one can, I repeat, allege weighty reasons for and against the system of subsidization. The reader understands that, in accordance with the special purpose of this essay, I have no need either to set forth these reasons or to decide between them.

But M. de Lamartine has advanced one argument that I cannot pass over in silence, for it falls within the very carefully defined limits of this economic study.

He has said:

The economic question in the matter of theaters can be summed up in one word: employment. The nature of the employment matters little; it is of a kind just as productive and fertile as any other kind. The theaters, as you know, support by wages no less than eighty thousand workers of all kinds—painters, masons, decorators, costumers, architects, etc., who are the very life and industry of many quarters of this capital, and they should have this claim upon your sympathies!

Your sympathies? Translate: your subsidies.

And further on:

---

† [This refers to the Great Exhibition, in Hyde Park, London, in 1851, sponsored by the London Society of Arts, an association devoted to the development of arts and industries. The first in a series of great international exhibitions, or "world fairs," it was famous for the Crystal Palace, a remarkable architectural structure, in which the exhibitions were displayed. Albert, Queen Victoria's Prince Consort, presided over the exhibition.—Translator.]

The pleasures of Paris provide employment and consumers' goods for the provincial departments, and the luxuries of the rich are the wages and the bread of two hundred thousand workers of all kinds, living on the complex industry of the theaters throughout the Republic, and receiving from these noble pleasures, which make France illustrious, their own livelihood and the means of providing the necessities of life for their families and their children. It is to them that you give these sixty thousand francs. [*Very good! Very good! Much applause.*]

For my part, I am forced to say: *Very bad! Very bad!* confining, of course, the burden of this judgment to the economic argument which we are here concerned with.

Yes, it is, at least in part, to the workers in the theaters that the sixty thousand francs in question will go. A few scraps might well get lost on the way. If one scrutinized the matter closely, one might even discover that most of the pie will find its way elsewhere. The workers will be fortunate if there are a few crumbs left for them! But I should like to assume that the entire subsidy will go to the painters, decorators, costumers, hairdressers, etc. *That is what is seen.*

But where does it come from? This is the *other side* of the coin, just as important to examine as its *face*. What is the source of these 60,000 francs? And where *would they have gone* if a legislative vote had not first directed them to the rue de Rivoli and from there to the rue de Grenelle?‡ *That is what is not seen.*

Surely, no one will dare maintain that the legislative vote has caused this sum to hatch out from the ballot box; that it is a pure addition to the national wealth; that, without this miraculous vote, these sixty thousand francs would have remained invisible and impalpable. It must be admitted that all that the majority can do is to decide that they will be taken from somewhere to be sent somewhere else, and that they will have one destination only by being deflected from another.

This being the case, it is clear that the taxpayer who will have been taxed one franc will no longer have this franc at his disposal. It is clear that he will be deprived of a satisfaction to the tune of one franc, and that the worker, whoever he is, who would have procured this satisfaction for him, will be deprived of wages in the same amount.

---

‡ [I.e., from City Hall to the theatrical suppliers on the Left Bank.—Translator.]

Let us not, then, yield to the childish illusion of believing that the vote of May 16 *adds* anything whatever to national well-being and employment. It reallocates possessions, it reallocates wages, and that is all.

Will it be said that for one kind of satisfaction and for one kind of job it substitutes satisfactions and jobs more urgent, more moral, more rational? I could do battle on this ground. I could say: In taking sixty thousand francs from the taxpayers, you reduce the wages of plowmen, ditchdiggers, carpenters, and blacksmiths, and you increase by the same amount the wages of singers, hairdressers, decorators, and costumers. Nothing proves that this latter class is more important than the other. M. de Lamartine does not make this allegation. He says himself that the work of the theaters is *just as* productive as, *just as* fruitful as, and not *more so* than, any other work, which might still be contested; for the best proof that theatrical work is not as productive as other work is that the latter is called upon to subsidize the former.

But this comparison of the intrinsic value and merit of the different kinds of work forms no part of my present subject. All that I have to do here is to show that, if M. de Lamartine and those who have applauded his argument have seen on the one hand the wages earned by those who supply the needs of the actors, they should see on the other the earnings lost by those who supply the needs of the taxpayers; if they do not, they are open to ridicule for mistaking a reallocation for a *gain*. If they were logical in their doctrine, they would ask for infinite subsidies; for what is true of one franc and of sixty thousand francs is true, in identical circumstances, of a billion francs.

When it is a question of taxes, gentlemen, prove their usefulness by reasons with some foundation, but not with that lamentable assertion: "Public spending keeps the working class alive." It makes the mistake of covering up a fact that it is essential to know: namely, that *public spending* is *always* a substitute for *private spending*, and that consequently it may well support one worker in place of another but adds nothing to the lot of the working class taken as a whole. Your argument is fashionable, but it is quite absurd, for the reasoning is not correct.

---

[3][See chap. 3 of *Economic Harmonies*.—Editor.]

Step 3

Hands-On Activity 1

<u>Experiential Learning</u>
Draw two BOT graphs and one CLD of Bastiat's description of "what is seen" and "what is not seen" in the economy when taxes subsidize theaters and fine arts.

Hands-On Activity 2

<u>Experiential Learning</u>
Find a news article about your local, state, or national government using taxes for subsidies and draw BOT graphs and CLDs of "what is seen" and "what is not seen" in the economy when this happens.

Activity 1 BOT: Theaters and Fine Arts Subsidies

What Is Seen	What Is NOT Seen

Unit 4: Theaters and Fine Arts

Activity 1 CLD

Activity 2 BOT

Activity 2 CLD

Step 4

Journal Writing

<u>Reflection and Synthesis</u>
Record in a journal your reactions to the learning.

Unit 4: Theaters and Fine Arts

Step 5

Evaluation Notes

Evaluation
Compare "what you saw" (your presumptions) with "what you did not see" (what you learned).

What I saw	What I did not see
1. I first saw..... .	1. But what I did not see was...

Unit 5: Public Works

Step 1

Free Writing

<u>Culturally-based presumptions</u>
Write what you think happens in the economy when taxes are used for public works.

Unit 5: Public Works

Step 2

Information Gap Writing

New knowledge
Read "Public Works." Compare your presumptions with what is learned.

Presumptions	New Knowledge	Information Gaps

Public Works

Nothing is more natural than that a nation, after making sure that a great enterprise will profit the community, should have such an enterprise carried out with funds collected from the citizenry. But I lose patience completely, I confess, when I hear alleged in support of such a resolution this economic fallacy: "Besides, it is a way of creating jobs for the workers."

The state opens a road, builds a palace, repairs a street, digs a canal; with these projects it gives jobs to certain workers. *That is what is seen.* But it deprives certain other laborers of employment. *That is what is not seen.*

Suppose a road is under construction. A thousand laborers arrive every morning, go home every evening, and receive their wages; that is certain. If the road had not been authorized, if funds for it had not been voted, these good people would have neither found this work nor earned these wages; that again is certain.

But is this all? Taken all together, does not the operation involve something else? At the moment when M. Dupin[*] pronounces the sacramental words: "The Assembly has adopted, ..." do millions of francs descend miraculously on a moonbeam into the coffers of M. Fould[†] and M. Bineau?[‡] For the process to be complete, does not the state have to organize the collection of funds as well as their expenditure? Does it not have to get its tax collectors into the country and its taxpayers to make their contribution?

Study the question, then, from its two aspects. In noting what the state is going to do with the millions of francs voted, do not neglect to note also what the taxpayers would have done—and can no longer do—with these same millions. You see, then, that a public enterprise is a coin with two sides. On one, the figure of a busy worker, with this device: *What is seen;* on the other, an unemployed worker, with this device: *What is not seen.*

---

[*] [Charles Dupin (1784–1873), distinguished French engineer and economist, professor at the Conservatory of Arts and Crafts, Deputy, and Senator. His greatest contribution to political economy was in the field of economic statistics.—Translator.]

[†] [Achille Fould (1800–1867), politician and financier.—Translator.]

[‡] [Jean Martial Bineau (1805–1855), engineer and politician, Minister of Finance in 1852.—Translator.]

The sophism that I am attacking in this essay is all the more dangerous when applied to public works, since it serves to justify the most foolishly prodigal enterprises. When a railroad or a bridge has real utility, it suffices to rely on this fact in arguing in its favor. But if one cannot do this, what does one do? One has recourse to this mumbo jumbo: "We must create jobs for the workers."

This means that the terraces of the Champ-de-Mars[§] are ordered first to be built up and then to be torn down. The great Napoleon, it is said, thought he was doing philanthropic work when he had ditches dug and then filled in. He also said: "What difference does the result make? All we need is to see wealth spread among the laboring classes."

Let us get to the bottom of things. Money creates an illusion for us. To ask for co-operation, in the form of money, from all the citizens in a common enterprise is, in reality, to ask of them actual physical co-operation, for each one of them procures for himself by his labor the amount he is taxed. Now, if we were to gather together all the citizens and exact their services from them in order to have a piece of work performed that is useful to all, this would be understandable; their recompense would consist in the results of the work itself. But if, after being brought together, they were forced to build roads on which no one would travel, or palaces that no one would live in, all under the pretext of providing work for them, it would seem absurd, and they would certainly be justified in objecting: We will have none of that kind of work. We would rather work for ourselves.

Having the citizens contribute money, and not labor, changes nothing in the general results. But if labor were contributed, the loss would be shared by everyone. Where money is contributed, those whom the state keeps busy escape their share of the loss, while adding much more to that which their compatriots already have to suffer.

There is an article in the Constitution which states:

[§] [Originally a parade ground in Paris on the Left Bank of the Seine, the Champ-de-Mars is now a park between the Eiffel Tower and the Military Academy.—Translator.]

"Society assists and encourages the development of labor.... through the establishment by the state, the departments, and the municipalities, of appropriate public works to employ idle hands."

As a temporary measure in a time of crisis, during a severe winter, this intervention on the part of the taxpayer could have good effects. It acts in the same way as insurance. It adds nothing to the number of jobs nor to total wages, but it takes labor and wages from ordinary times and doles them out, at a loss it is true, in difficult times.

As a permanent, general, systematic measure, it is nothing but a ruinous hoax, an impossibility, a contradiction, which makes a great show of the little work that it has stimulated, which is *what is seen,* and conceals the much larger amount of work that it has precluded, which is *what is not seen.*

Unit 5: Public Works

Step 3

Hands-On Activity 1

Experiential Learning
Draw two BOT graphs and one CLD of Bastiat's description of "what is seen" and "what is not seen" in the economy when taxes are used for public works.

Hands-On Activity 2

Experiential Learning
Find a news article about your local, state, or national government using taxes for a public works project and draw BOT graphs and CLDs of "what is seen" and "what is not seen" in the economy when this happens.

Activity 1 BOT: Public Works

What Is Seen	What Is NOT Seen

Activity 1 CLD

Activity 2 BOT

Unit 5: Public Works

Activity 2 CLD

Step 4

Journal Writing

<u>Reflection and Synthesis</u>
Record in a journal your reactions to the learning.

Step 5

Evaluation Notes

Evaluation
Compare "what you saw" (your presumptions) with "what you did not see" (what you learned).

What I saw	What I did not see
1. I first saw..... .	1. But what I did not see was...

Unit 6: The Middlemen

> ## Step 1
>
> ## Free Writing
>
> Culturally-based presumptions
> Write what you think happens in the economy when private services are nationalized.

Step 2

Information Gap Writing

<u>New knowledge</u>
Read "The Middlemen." Compare your presumptions with what is learned.

Presumptions	New Knowledge	Information Gaps

The Middlemen

Society is the aggregate of all the services that men perform for one another by compulsion or voluntarily, that is to say, *public services* and *private services*.

The first, imposed and regulated by the law, which is not always easy to change when necessary, can long outlive their usefulness and still retain the name of *public services,* even when they are no longer anything but public nuisances. The second are in the domain of the voluntary, i.e., of individual responsibility. Each gives and receives what he wishes, or what he can, after bargaining. These services are always presumed to have a real utility, exactly measured by their comparative value.

That is why the former are so often static, while the latter obey the law of progress.

While the exaggerated development of public services, with the waste of energies that it entails, tends to create a disastrous parasitism in society, it is rather strange that many modern schools of economic thought, attributing this characteristic to voluntary, private services, seek to transform the functions performed by the various occupations.

These schools of thought are vehement in their attack on those they call middlemen. They would willingly eliminate the capitalist, the banker, the speculator, the entrepreneur, the businessman, and the merchant, accusing them of interposing themselves between producer and consumer in order to fleece them both, without giving them anything of value. Or rather, the reformers would like to transfer to the state the work of the middlemen, for this work cannot be eliminated.

The sophism of the socialists on this point consists in showing the public what it pays to the *middlemen* for their services and in concealing what would have to be paid to the state. Once again we have the conflict between what strikes the eye and what is evidenced only to the mind, between *what is seen and what is not seen.*

It was especially in 1847 and on the occasion of the famine* that the socialist schools succeeded in popularizing their disastrous theory. They knew well that the most absurd propaganda always has some chance with men who are suffering; *malesuada fames*.†

Then, with the aid of those high-sounding words: *Exploitation of man by man, speculation in hunger, monopoly*, they set themselves to blackening the name of business and throwing a veil over its benefits.

"Why," they said, "leave to merchants the task of getting foodstuffs from the United States and the Crimea? Why cannot the state, the departments, and the municipalities organize a provisioning service and set up warehouses for stockpiling? They would sell at *net cost*, and the people, the poor people, would be relieved of the tribute that they pay to free, i.e., selfish, individualistic, anarchical trade."

The tribute that the people pay to business, *is what is seen*. The tribute that the people would have to pay to the state or to its agents in the socialist system, *is what is not seen*.

What is this so-called tribute that people pay to business? It is this: that two men render each other a service in full freedom under the pressure of competition and at a price agreed on after bargaining.

When the stomach that is hungry is in Paris and the wheat that can satisfy it is in Odessa, the suffering will not cease until the wheat reaches the stomach. There are three ways to accomplish this: the hungry men can go themselves to find the wheat; they can put their trust in those who engage in this kind of business; or they can levy an assessment on themselves and charge public officials with the task.

Of these three methods, which is the most advantageous?

In all times, in all countries, the freer, the more enlightened, the more experienced men have been, the oftener have they *voluntarily* chosen the second. I confess that this is enough in my eyes to give the

---

* [Failures in the grain and potato crops in northern and western Europe in 1846 resulted in a rise of food prices in 1847, the year of "dear bread" and of agricultural, industrial, and financial depressions.—Translator.]

† ["Hunger is an evil counsellor." Virgil's *Aeneid* VI, 276.—Translator.]

advantage to it. My mind refuses to admit that mankind at large deceives itself on a point that touches it so closely.[4]

However, let us examine the question.

For thirty-six million citizens to depart for Odessa to get the wheat that they need is obviously impracticable. The first means is of no avail. The consumers cannot act by themselves; they are compelled to turn to middlemen, whether public officials or merchants.

However, let us observe that the first means would be the most natural. Fundamentally, it is the responsibility of whoever is hungry to get his own wheat. It is a *task* that concerns him; it is a *service* that he owes to himself. If someone else, whoever he may be, performs this *service* for him and takes the task on himself, this other person has a right to compensation. What I am saying here is that the services of *middlemen* involve a right to remuneration.

However that may be, since we must turn to what the socialists call a parasite, which of the two—the merchant or the public official—is the less demanding parasite?

Business (I assume it to be free, or else what point would there be in my argument?) is forced, by its own self-interest, to study the seasons, to ascertain day by day the condition of the crops, to receive reports from all parts of the world, to foresee needs, to take precautions. It has ships all ready, associates everywhere, and its immediate self-interest is to buy at the lowest possible price, to economize on all details of operation, and to attain the greatest results with the least effort. Not only French merchants, but merchants the whole world over are busy with provisioning France for the day of need; and if self-interest compels them to fulfill their task at the least expense, competition among them no less compels them to let the consumers profit from all the economies realized. Once the wheat has arrived, the businessman has an interest in selling it as soon as possible to cover his risks, realize his profits, and begin all over again, if there is an opportunity. Guided by the comparison of prices, private enterprise distributes food all over the world, always beginning at the point of greatest scarcity, that is, where the need is felt the most. It is thus impossible to imagine an *organization* better calculated to serve the interests of the hungry, and the beauty of this organization, not perceived by the socialists, comes precisely from the fact that it is free, i.e., voluntary. True, the consumer must pay the businessman for his expenses of cartage, of trans-shipment, of storage, of commissions, etc.; but under what system does the one who consumes the wheat avoid paying the expenses of shipping it to him? There is, besides, the necessity of paying also for *service rendered*; but, so far as the share of the middleman is concerned, it is reduced to a *minimum* by competition; and as to its justice, it would be strange for the artisans of Paris not to work for the merchants of Marseilles, when the merchants of Marseilles work for the artisans of Paris.

If, according to the socialist plan, the state takes the place of private businessmen in these transactions, what will happen? Pray, show me where there will be any economy for the public. Will it be in the retail price? But imagine the representatives of forty thousand municipalities arriving at Odessa on a given day, the day when the wheat is needed; imagine the effect on the price. Will the economy be effected in the shipping expenses? But will fewer ships, fewer sailors, fewer trans-shipments, fewer warehouses be needed, or are we to be relieved of the necessity for paying for all these things? Will the saving be effected in the profits of the businessmen? But did your representatives and public officials go to Odessa for nothing? Are they going to make the journey out of brotherly love? Will they not have to live? Will not their time have to be paid for? And do you think that this will not exceed a thousand times the two or three per cent that the merchant earns, a rate that he is prepared to guarantee?

And then, think of the difficulty of levying so many taxes to distribute so much food. Think of the injustices and abuses inseparable from such an enterprise. Think of the burden of responsibility that the government would have to bear.

The socialists who have invented these follies, and who in days of distress plant them in the minds of the masses, generously confer on themselves the title of "forward-looking" men, and there is a real danger that usage, that tyrant of language, will ratify both the word and the judgment it implies. "Forward-looking" assumes that these gentlemen can see ahead much further than ordinary people; that their only fault is to be too much in advance of their century; and that, if the time has not yet arrived when certain private services, allegedly parasitical, can be eliminated, the fault is with the public, which is far behind socialism. To *my* mind and knowledge, it is the contrary that is true, and I do not know to what barbaric century we should have to return to find on this point a level of understanding comparable to that of the socialists.

Unit 6: The Middlemen

The modern socialist factions ceaselessly oppose free association in present-day society. They do not realize that a free society is a true association much superior to any of those that they concoct out of their fertile imaginations.

Let us elucidate this point with an example:

For a man, when he gets up in the morning, to be able to put on a suit of clothes, a piece of land has had to be enclosed, fertilized, drained, cultivated, planted with a certain kind of vegetation; flocks of sheep have had to feed on it; they have had to give their wool; this wool has had to be spun, woven, dyed, and converted into cloth; this cloth has had to be cut, sewn, and fashioned into a garment. And this series of operations implies a host of others; for it presupposes the use of farming implements, of sheepfolds, of factories, of coal, of machines, of carriages, etc.

If society were not a very real association, anyone who wanted a suit of clothes would be reduced to working in isolation, that is, to performing himself the innumerable operations in this series, from the first blow of the pickaxe that initiates it right down to the last thrust of the needle that terminates it.

But thanks to that readiness to associate which is the distinctive characteristic of our species, these operations have been distributed among a multitude of workers, and they keep subdividing themselves more and more for the common good to the point where, as consumption increases, a single specialized operation can support a new industry. Then comes the distribution of the proceeds, according to the portion of value each one has contributed to the total work. If this is not association, I should like to know what is.

Note that, since not one of the workers has produced the smallest particle of raw material from nothing, they are confined to rendering each other mutual services, to aiding each other for a common end; and that all can be considered, each group in relation to the others, as *middlemen*. If, for example, in the course of the operation, transportation becomes important enough to employ one person; spinning, a second; weaving, a third; why should the first one be considered more of a *parasite* than the others? Is there no need for transportation? Does not

67

someone devote time and trouble to the task? Does he not spare his associates this time and trouble? Are they doing more than he, or just something different? Are they not all equally subject, in regard to their pay, that is, their share of the proceeds, to the law that restricts it to the *price agreed upon after bargaining*? Do not this division of labor and these arrangements, decided upon in full liberty, serve the common good? Do we, then, need a socialist, under the pretext of planning, to come and despotically destroy our voluntary arrangements, put an end to the division of labor, substitute isolated efforts for co-operative efforts, and reverse the progress of civilization?

Is association as I describe it here any the less association because everyone enters and leaves it voluntarily, chooses his place in it, judges and bargains for himself, under his own responsibility, and brings to it the force and the assurance of his own self-interest? For association to deserve the name, does a so-called reformer have to come and impose his formula and his will on us and concentrate within himself, so to speak, all of mankind?

The more one examines these "forward-looking" schools of thought, the more one is convinced that at bottom they rest on nothing but ignorance proclaiming itself infallible and demanding despotic power in the name of this infallibility.

I hope that the reader will excuse this digression. It is perhaps not entirely useless at the moment when, coming straight from the books of the Saint-Simonians, of the advocates of phalansteries, and of the admirers of Icaria[‡], tirades against the middlemen fill the press and the Assembly and seriously menace the freedom of labor and exchange.

---

[4] The author has often invoked the presumption of truth which is connected with the *universal assent* manifested by the practice of all men. See especially chap. 13 of *Economic Sophisms*, the end of chap. 6 of the *Essays* (in the French edition), and in *Economic Harmonies* the appendix to chap. 6 entitled "Morality of Wealth."—Editor.]

[‡] [References to Claude Henri de Rouvroy, Comte de Saint-Simon (1760–1825), historic founder of French socialism; to the phalanstères, or common buildings, proposed by Francois Marie Charles Fourier in 1832 in his newspaper *Le Phalanstère* to house "phalanges" of sixteen hundred persons each as part of a socialistic scheme; and to *Voyage to Icaria,* a utopian book by Étienne Cabet (1788–1856).—Translator.]

Unit 6: The Middlemen

Step 3

Hands-On Activity 1

<u>Experiential Learning</u>
Draw two BOT graphs, one for middlemen acting in a free market and one for the nationalization of the middlemen. In addition, draw two CLDs of Bastiat's description of "what is seen" and "what is not seen" in the economy when middlemen are free and when they are nationalized.

Hands-On Activity 2

<u>Experiential Learning</u>
Find a news article about the nationalization of the US housing industry (people's foreclosed homes), General Motors, or Lloyds of London and draw a BOT graph and CLDs of "what is seen" and "what is not seen" in the economy as a result of nationalization.

Activity 1 BOT: Middlemen	
Free Market	*Nationalization*

Activity 1 CLD

| Free Market | Nationalization |

Activity 2 BOT

Unit 6: The Middlemen

Activity 2 CLD

Step 4

Journal Writing

<u>Reflection and Synthesis</u>
Record in a journal your reactions to the learning.

Step 5

Evaluation Notes

Evaluation
Compare "what you saw" (your presumptions) with "what you did not see" (what you learned).

What I saw	What I did not see
1. I first saw..... .	1. But what I did not see was...

Unit 7: Restraint of Trade

Step 1

Free Writing

<u>Culturally-based presumptions</u>
Write what you think happens in the economy when protectionist laws are imposed by a national legislature.

Step 2

Information Gap Writing

<u>New knowledge</u>
Read "Restraint of Trade." Compare your presumptions with what is learned.

Presumptions	New Knowledge	Information Gaps

Restraint of Trade

Mr. Protectionist[*] (it was not I who gave him that name; it was M. Charles Dupin) devoted his time and his capital to converting ore from his lands into iron. Since Nature had been more generous with the Belgians, they sold iron to the French at a better price than Mr. Protectionist did, which meant that all Frenchmen, or France, could obtain a given quantity of iron *with less labor* by buying it from the good people of Flanders. Therefore, prompted by their self-interest, they took full advantage of the situation, and every day a multitude of nailmakers, metalworkers, cartwrights, mechanics, blacksmiths, and plowmen could be seen either going themselves or sending middlemen to Belgium to obtain their supply of iron. Mr. Protectionist did not like this at all.

His first idea was to stop this abuse by direct intervention with his own two hands. This was certainly the least he could do, since he alone was harmed. I'll take my carbine, he said to himself. I'll put four pistols in my belt, I'll fill my cartridge box, I'll buckle on my sword, and, thus equipped, I'll go to the frontier. There I'll kill the first metalworker, nailmaker, blacksmith, mechanic, or locksmith who comes seeking his own profit rather than mine. That'll teach him a lesson!

At the moment of leaving, Mr. Protectionist had a few second thoughts that somewhat tempered his bellicose ardor. He said to himself: First of all, it is quite possible that the buyers of iron, my fellow countrymen and my enemies, will take offense, and, instead of letting themselves be killed, they might kill me. Furthermore, even if all my servants marched out, we could not guard the whole frontier. Finally, the entire proceeding would cost me too much, more than the result would be worth.

Mr. Protectionist was going to resign himself sadly just to being free like everyone else, when suddenly he had a brilliant idea.

He remembered that there is a great law factory in Paris. What is a law? he asked himself. It is a measure to which, when once promulgated, whether it is good or bad, everyone has to

---

[*] In French, *"M. Prohibant"*: this ironic term for a protectionist, coined, as Bastiat says, by Charles Dupin, could be roughly translated as "Mr. Restrainer-of-Trade" or "Mr. Protectionist."—Translator.]

conform. For the execution of this law, a public police force is organized, and to make up the said public police force, men and money are taken from the nation.

If, then, I manage to get from that great Parisian factory a nice little law saying: "Belgian iron is prohibited," I shall attain the following results: The government will replace the few servants that I wanted to send to the frontier with twenty thousand sons of my recalcitrant metalworkers, locksmiths, nailmakers, blacksmiths, artisans, mechanics, and plowmen. Then, to keep these twenty thousand customs officers in good spirits and health, there will be distributed to them twenty-five million francs taken from these same blacksmiths, nailmakers, artisans, and plowmen. Organized in this way, the protection will be better accomplished; it will cost me nothing; I shall not be exposed to the brutality of brokers; I shall sell the iron at my price; and I shall enjoy the sweet pleasure of seeing our great people shamefully hoaxed. That will teach them to be continually proclaiming themselves the precursors and the promoters of all progress in Europe. It will be a smart move, and well worth the trouble of trying!

So Mr. Protectionist went to the law factory. (Another time, perhaps, I shall tell the story of his dark, underhanded dealings there; today I wish to speak only of the steps he took openly and for all to see.) He presented to their excellencies, the legislators, the following argument:

"Belgian iron is sold in France at ten francs, which forces me to sell mine at the same price. I should prefer to sell it at fifteen and cannot because of this confounded Belgian iron. Manufacture a law that says: 'Belgian iron shall no longer enter France.' Immediately I shall raise my price by five francs, with the following consequences:

"For each hundred kilograms of iron that I shall deliver to the public, instead of ten francs I shall get fifteen; I shall enrich myself more quickly; I shall extend the exploitation of my mines; I shall employ more men. My employees and I will spend more, to the great advantage of our suppliers for miles around. These suppliers, having a greater market, will give more orders to industry, and gradually this activity will spread throughout the country. This lucky hundred-sou piece that you will drop into my coffers, like a stone that is thrown into a lake, will cause an infinite number of concentric circles to radiate great distances in every direction."

Charmed by this discourse, enchanted to learn that it is so easy to increase the wealth of a people simply by legislation, the manufacturers of laws voted in favor of the restriction. "What is all this talk about labor and saving?" they said. "What good are these painful means of increasing the national wealth, when a decree will do the job?"

And, in fact, the law had all the consequences predicted by Mr. Protectionist, but it had others too; for, to do him justice, he had not reasoned *falsely*, but *incompletely*. In asking for a privilege, he had pointed out the effects *that are seen*, leaving in the shadow those *that are not seen*. He had shown only two people, when actually there are three in the picture. It is for us to repair this omission, whether involuntary or premeditated.

Yes, the five-franc piece thus legislatively rechanneled into the coffers of Mr. Protectionist constitutes an advantage for him and for those who get jobs because of it. And if the decree had made the five-franc piece come down from the moon, these good effects would not be counterbalanced by any compensating bad effects. Unfortunately, the mysterious hundred sous did not come down from the moon, but rather from the pocket of a metalworker, a nailmaker, a cartwright, a blacksmith, a plowman, a builder, in a word, from James Goodfellow, who pays it out today without receiving a milligram of iron more than when he was paying ten francs. It at once becomes evident that this certainly changes the question, for, quite obviously, the *profit* of Mr. Protectionist is counterbalanced by the *loss* of James Goodfellow, and anything that Mr. Protectionist will be able to do with this five-franc piece for the encouragement of domestic industry, James Goodfellow could also have done. The stone is thrown in at one point in the lake only because it has been prohibited by law from being thrown in at another.

Hence, *what is not seen* counterbalances *what is seen;* and the outcome of the whole operation is an injustice, all the more deplorable in having been perpetrated by the law.

But this is not all. I have said that a third person was always left in the shadow. I must make him appear here, so that he can reveal to us a *second loss* of five francs. Then we shall have the results of the operation in its entirety.

James Goodfellow has fifteen francs, the fruit of his labors. (We are back at the time when he is still free.) What does he do with his fifteen francs? He buys an article of millinery for ten francs, and it is with this article of millinery that he pays (or his middleman pays for him) for the hundred kilograms of Belgian iron. He still has five francs left. He does not throw them into the river, but (and this is *what is not seen*) he gives them to some manufacturer or other in exchange for some satisfaction—for example, to a publisher for a copy of the *Discourse on Universal History by Bossuet.*†

Thus, he has encouraged *domestic industry* to the amount of fifteen francs, to wit:

10 francs to the Parisian milliner
5 francs to the publisher

And as for James Goodfellow, he gets for his fifteen francs two objects of satisfaction, to wit:

1. A hundred kilograms of iron
2. A book

Comes the decree.

What happens to James Goodfellow? What happens to domestic industry?

James Goodfellow, in giving his fifteen francs to the last centime to Mr. Protectionist for a hundred kilograms of iron, has nothing now but the use of this iron. He loses the enjoyment of a book or of any other equivalent object. He loses five francs. You agree with this; you cannot fail to agree; you cannot fail to agree that when restraint of trade raises prices, the consumer loses the difference.

But it is said that *domestic industry* gains the difference.

---

† [Jacques Bénigne Bossuet (1627–1704), bishop of Condom and of Meaux, was the outstanding pulpit orator of his day, his funeral orations for members of the royal family ranking as brilliant examples of French classical style and power. As tutor to the heir apparent, the son of Louis XIV, he wrote his *Histoire universelle*, one of the classics on which French school children were raised for generations. His vigorous stand against Protestantism and his successful leadership of the Gallican movement, which brought increased independence to the French Catholic Church, reveal him as an important ecclesiastical, as well as literary, figure.—Translator.]

No, it does not gain it; for, since the decree, it is encouraged only as much as it was before, to the amount of fifteen francs.

Only, since the decree, the fifteen francs of James Goodfellow go to metallurgy, while before the decree they were divided between millinery and publishing.

The force that Mr. Protectionist might exercise by himself at the frontier and that which he has the law exercise for him can be judged quite differently from the moral point of view. There are people who think that plunder loses all its immorality as soon as it becomes legal. Personally, I cannot imagine a more alarming situation. However that may be, one thing is certain, and that is that the economic results are the same.

You may look at the question from any point of view you like, but if you examine it dispassionately, you will see that no good can come from legal or illegal plunder. We do not deny that it may bring for Mr. Protectionist or his industry, or if you wish for domestic industry, a profit of five francs. But we affirm that it will also give rise to two losses: one for James Goodfellow, who pays fifteen francs for what he used to get for ten; the other for domestic industry, which no longer receives the difference. Make your own choice of which of these two losses compensates for the profit that we admit. The one you do not choose constitutes no less a *dead loss*.

Moral: To use force is not to produce, but to destroy. Heavens! If to use force were to produce, France would be much richer than she is.

What Is Seen and What Is Not Seen: Fun Systems Thinking Activities with Frédéric Bastiat

Step 3

Hands-On Activity 1

<u>Experiential Learning</u>
Draw two BOT graphs and one CLD of Bastiat's description of "what is seen" and "what is not seen" in the economy when the national legislature makes it illegal for French to purchase Belgian iron.

Hands-On Activity 2

<u>Experiential Learning</u>
Find a news article about a national legislature raising import tariffs on a foreign good and draw a BOT graph and CLDs of the effect this has on the economy.

Activity 1 BOT: Restraint of Trade

Free Market	*Belgian Iron Forbidden*

Unit 7: Restraint of Trade

Activity 1 CLD

Activity 2 BOT

Activity 2 CLD

Step 4

Journal Writing

<u>Reflection and Synthesis</u>
Record in a journal your reactions to the learning.

Unit 7: Restraint of Trade

Step 5
Evaluation Notes

Evaluation
Compare "what you saw" (your presumptions) with "what you did not see" (what you learned).

What I saw	What I did not see
1. I first saw….. .	1. But what I did not see was…

Unit 8: Machines

Step 1

Free Writing

<u>Culturally-based presumptions</u>
Write what you think happens in the economy when a government forbids the use of a technology.

Unit 8: Machines

Step 2

Information Gap Writing

<u>New knowledge</u>
Read "Machines." Compare your presumptions with what is learned.

Presumptions	New Knowledge	Information Gaps

Machines

"A curse on machines! Every year their increasing power condemns to pauperism millions of workers, taking their jobs away from them, and with their jobs their wages, and with their wages their bread! A curse on machines!"

That is the cry rising from ignorant prejudice, and whose echo resounds in the newspapers.

But to curse machines is to curse the human mind!

What puzzles me is that it is possible to find anyone at all who can be content with such a doctrine.[5]

For, in the last analysis, if it is true, what is its strictly logical consequence? It is that activity, well-being, wealth, and happiness are possible only for stupid nations, mentally static, to whom God has not given the disastrous gift of thinking, observing, contriving, inventing, obtaining the greatest results with the least trouble. On the contrary, rags, miserable huts, poverty, and stagnation are the inevitable portion of every nation that looks for and finds in iron, fire, wind, electricity, magnetism, the laws of chemistry and mechanics—in a word, in the forces of Nature—an addition to its own resources, and it is indeed appropriate to say with Rousseau: "Every man who thinks is a depraved animal."

But this is not all. If this doctrine is true, and as all men think and invent, as all, in fact, from first to last, and at every minute of their existence, seek to make the forces of Nature co-operate with them, to do more with less, to reduce their own manual labor or that of those whom they pay, to attain the greatest possible sum of satisfactions with the least possible amount of work; we must conclude that all mankind is on the way to decadence, precisely because of this intelligent aspiration towards progress that seems to torment every one of its members.

Hence, it would have to be established statistically that the inhabitants of Lancaster, fleeing that machine-ridden country, go in search of employment to Ireland, where machines are unknown; and, historically, that the shadow of barbarism darkens the epochs of civilization, and that civilization flourishes in times of ignorance and barbarism.

Unit 8: Machines

Evidently there is in this mass of contradictions something that shocks us and warns us that the problem conceals an element essential to its solution that has not been sufficiently brought to light.

The whole mystery consists in this: behind *what is seen* lies *what is not seen*. I am going to try to shed some light on it. My demonstration can be nothing but a repetition of the preceding one, for the problem is the same.

Men have a natural inclination, if they are not prevented by force, to go for a *bargain*—that is, for something that, for an equivalent satisfaction, spares them labor—whether this bargain comes to them from a capable *foreign producer* or from a capable *mechanical producer*.

The theoretical objection that is raised against this inclination is the same in both cases. In one as in the other, the reproach is made that it apparently makes for a scarcity of jobs. However, its actual effect is not to make jobs scarce, but to *free* men's labor for other jobs.

And that is why, in practice, the same obstacle—force—is set up against it in both cases. The legislator *prohibits* foreign competition and *forbids* mechanical competition. For what other means can there be to stifle an inclination natural to all men than to take away their freedom?

In many countries, it is true, the legislator strikes at only one of these types of competition and confines himself to grumbling about the other. This proves only that in these countries the legislator is inconsistent.

That should not surprise us. On a false path there is always inconsistency; if this were not so, mankind would be destroyed. We have never seen and never shall see a false principle carried out completely. I have said elsewhere: Absurdity is the limit of inconsistency. I should like to add: It is also its proof.

Let us go on with our demonstration; it will not be lengthy.

James Goodfellow had two francs that he let two workers earn.

But now suppose that he devises an arrangement of ropes and weights that will shorten the work by half.

Then he obtains the same satisfaction, saves a franc, and discharges a worker.

He discharges a worker: *that is what is seen*.

Seeing only this, people say: "See how misery follows civilization! See how freedom is fatal to equality! The human mind has made a conquest, and immediately another worker has forever fallen into the abyss of poverty. Perhaps James Goodfellow can still continue to have both men work for him, but he cannot give them more than ten sous each, for they will compete with one another and will offer their services at a lower rate. This is how the rich get richer and the poor become poorer. We must remake society."

A fine conclusion, and one worthy of the initial premise!

Fortunately, both premise and conclusion are false, because behind the half of the phenomenon *that is seen* is the other half *that is not seen*.

The franc saved by James Goodfellow and the necessary effects of this saving are not seen.

Since, as a result of his own invention, James Goodfellow no longer spends more than one franc for manual labor in the pursuit of a given satisfaction, he has another franc left over.

If, then, there is somewhere an idle worker who offers his labor on the market, there is also somewhere a capitalist who offers his idle franc. These two elements meet and combine.

And it is clear as day that between the supply of and the demand for labor, between the supply of and the demand for wages, the relationship has in no way changed.

The invention and the worker, paid with the first franc, now do the work previously accomplished by two workers.

The second worker, paid with the second franc, performs some new work.

What has then been changed in the world? There is one national satisfaction the more; in other words, the invention is a gratuitous conquest, a gratuitous profit for mankind.

From the form in which I have given my demonstration we could draw this conclusion:

"It is the capitalist who derives all the benefits flowing from the invention of machines. The laboring class, even though it suffers from them only temporarily, never profits from them, since, according to what you yourself say, they *reallocate* a portion of the nation's industry without *diminishing* it, it is true, but also without *increasing* it."

It is not within the province of this essay to answer all objections. Its only object is to combat an ignorant prejudice, very dangerous and extremely widespread. I wished to prove that a new machine, in making a certain number of workers available for jobs, *necessarily* makes available at the same time the money that pays them. These workers and this money get together eventually to produce something that was impossible to produce before the invention; from which it follows that *the final result of the invention is an increase in satisfactions with the same amount of labor.*

Who reaps this excess of satisfactions?

Yes, at first it is the capitalist, the inventor, the first one who uses the machine successfully, and this is the reward for his genius and daring. In this case, as we have just seen, he realizes a saving on the costs of production, which, no matter how it is spent (and it always is), gives employment to just as many hands as the machine has made idle.

But soon competition forces him to lower his selling price by the amount of this saving itself.

And then it is no longer the inventor who reaps the benefits of the invention; it is the buyer of the product, the consumer, the public, including the workers—in a word, it is mankind.

And *what is not seen* is that the saving, thus procured for all the consumers, forms a fund from which wages can be drawn, replacing what the machine has drained off.

Thus (taking up again the foregoing example), James Goodfellow obtains a product by spending two francs for wages.

Thanks to his invention, the manual labor now costs him only one franc.

As long as he sells the product at the same price, there is one worker the fewer employed in making this special product: *that is what is seen;* but there is one worker the more employed by the franc James Goodfellow has saved: *that is what is not seen.*

When, in the natural course of events, James Goodfellow is reduced to lowering by one franc the price of the product, he no longer realizes a saving; then he no longer releases a franc for national employment in new production. But whoever acquires it, i.e., mankind, takes his place. Whoever buys the product pays one franc less, saves a franc, and necessarily hands over this saving to the fund for wages; this is again *what is not seen.*

Another solution to this problem, one founded on the facts, has been advanced.

Some have said: "The machine reduces the expenses of production and lowers the price of the product. The lowering of the price stimulates an increase in consumption, which necessitates an increase in production, and, finally, the use of as many workers as before the invention—or more." In support of this argument they cite printing, spinning, the press, etc.

This demonstration is not scientific.

We should have to conclude from it that, if the consumption of the special product in question remains stationary or nearly so, the machine will be harmful to employment. This is not so.

Suppose that in a certain country all the men wear hats. If with a machine the price of hats can be reduced by half, it does not *necessarily* follow that twice as many hats will be bought.

Will it be said, in that case, that a part of the national labor force has been made idle? Yes, according to ignorant reasoning. No, according to mine; for, even though in that country no one were to buy a single extra hat, the entire fund for wages would nevertheless remain intact; whatever did not go to the hat industry would be found in the saving realized by all consumers and would go to pay wages for the whole of the labor force that the machine had rendered unnecessary and to stimulate a new development of all industries.

And this is, in fact, the way things happen. I have seen newspapers at 80 francs; now they sell for 48. This is a saving of 32 francs for the subscribers. It is not certain, at least it is not inevitable, that the 32 francs continue to go into journalism; but what is certain, what is inevitable, is that, if they do not take this direction, they will take another. One franc will be used to buy more newspapers, another for more food, a third for better clothes, a fourth for better furniture.

Thus, all industries are interrelated. They form a vast network in which all the lines communicate by secret channels. What is saved in one profits all. What is important is to understand clearly that never, never are economies effected at the expense of jobs and wages.[6]

---

[5] [See in Vol. V, pages 86 and 94 (of the French edition), chaps. 14 and 18 of the first series of *Economic Sophisms*, as well as chap. 7 (of this volume).—Editor.]

[6] [See in *Economic Harmonies* chaps. 3 and 8.—Editor.]

Step 3

Hands-On Activity 1

Experiential Learning

Draw two BOT graphs, one showing technological innovation in a free market economy and one where technology is restrained by government. Also draw two CLDs of Bastiat's description of "what is seen" and "what is not seen" in the economy with technological innovation, one CLD from an employment perspective and another CLD from a consumer perspective.

Hands-On Activity 2

Experiential Learning

Find a news article about the Google-Chinese government controversy or another private enterprise-government controversy restricting the use of technology and draw BOT graphs and CLDs of "what is seen" and "what is not seen" in the economy as a result of the government restrictions.

Activity 1 BOT: **Machines** *Free Market*	*Technology Restrained by Government*

Unit 8: Machines

Activity 1 CLD	
Employment Perspective	Consumer Perspective

Activity 2 BOT

93

Activity 2 CLD

Step 4

Journal Writing

Reflection and Synthesis
Record in a journal your reactions to the learning.

Unit 8: Machines

Step 5
Evaluation Notes

Evaluation
Compare "what you saw" (your presumptions) with "what you did not see" (what you learned).

What I saw	What I did not see
1. I first saw..... .	1. But what I did not see was...

Unit 9: Credit

Step 1

Free Writing

<u>Culturally-based presumptions</u>
Write what you think happens in the economy when a government universalizes credit, meaning, loan defaults on both the principal and interest of loans are guaranteed by government.

Unit 9: Credit

Step 2

Information Gap Writing

<u>New knowledge</u>
Read "Credit." Compare your presumptions with what is learned.

Presumptions	New Knowledge	Information Gaps

97

Credit

At all times, but especially in the last few years, people have dreamt of universalizing wealth by universalizing credit.

I am sure I do not exaggerate in saying that since the February Revolution* the Paris presses have spewed forth more than ten thousand brochures extolling this solution of the *social problem.*

This solution, alas, has as its foundation merely an optical illusion, in so far as an illusion can serve as a foundation for anything.

These people begin by confusing hard money with products; then they confuse paper money with hard money; and it is from these two confusions that they profess to derive a fact.

In this question it is absolutely necessary to forget money, coins, bank notes, and the other media by which products pass from hand to hand, in order to see only the products themselves, which constitute the real substance of a loan.

For when a farmer borrows fifty francs to buy a plow, it is not actually the fifty francs that is lent to him; it is the plow.

And when a merchant borrows twenty thousand francs to buy a house, it is not the twenty thousand francs he owes; it is the house.

Money makes its appearance only to facilitate the arrangement among several parties.
Peter may not be disposed to lend his plow, but James may be willing to lend his money. What does William do then? He borrows the money from James, and with this money he buys the plow from Peter.

---

* [Popular demonstrations against Prime Minister Guizot on February 22, 1848, resulted in his dismissal by King Louis Philippe. This prudent move, however, proved unavailing for the King, because the next day troops fired on a group of demonstrators, and the people of Paris responded with an armed revolt, which brought about the abdication of Louis Philippe and the establishment of the Second Republic.—Translator.]

But actually nobody borrows money for the sake of the money itself. We borrow money to get products.

Now, in no country is it possible to transfer from one hand to another more products than there are.

Whatever the sum of hard money and bills that circulates, the borrowers taken together cannot get more plows, houses, tools, provisions, or raw materials than the total number of lenders can furnish.

For let us keep well in mind that every borrower presupposes a lender, that every borrowing implies a loan.

This much being granted, what good can credit institutions do? They can make it easier for borrowers and lenders to find one another and reach an understanding. But what they cannot do is to increase instantaneously the total number of objects borrowed and lent.

However, the credit organizations would have to do just this in order for the end of the social reformers to be attained, since these gentlemen aspire to nothing less than to give plows, houses, tools, provisions, and raw materials to everyone who wants them.

And how do they imagine they will do this?

By giving to loans the guarantee of the state.

Let us go more deeply into the matter, for there is something here that is *seen* and something that *is not seen*. Let us try to see both.

Suppose that there is only one plow in the world and that two farmers want it.

Peter is the owner of the only plow available in France. John and James wish to borrow it. John, with his honesty, his property, and his good name, offers guarantees. One *believes* in him;

he has *credit*. James does not inspire confidence or at any rate seems less reliable. Naturally, Peter lends his plow to John.

But now, under socialist inspiration, the state intervenes and says to Peter: "Lend your plow to James. We will guarantee you reimbursement, and this guarantee is worth more than John's, for he is the only one responsible for himself, and we, though it is true we have nothing, dispose of the wealth of all the taxpayers; if necessary, we will pay back the principal and the interest with their money."

So Peter lends his plow to James; *this is what is seen*.

And the socialists congratulate themselves, saying, "See how our plan has succeeded. Thanks to the intervention of the state, poor James has a plow. He no longer has to spade by hand; he is on the way to making his fortune. It is a benefit for him and a profit for the nation as a whole."

Oh no, gentlemen, it is not a profit for the nation, for here is *what is not seen*.

It is not seen that the plow goes to James because it did not go to John.

It is not seen that if James pushes a plow instead of spading, John will be reduced to spading instead of plowing.

Consequently, what one would like to think of as an *additional* loan is only the *reallocation* of a loan.

Furthermore, *it is not seen* that this reallocation involves two profound injustices: injustice to John, who, after having merited and won *credit* by his honesty and his energy, sees himself deprived; injustice to the taxpayers, obligated to pay a debt that does not concern them.

Will it be said that the government offers to John the same opportunities it does to James? But since there is only one plow available, two cannot be lent. The argument always comes back to the statement that, thanks to the intervention of the state, more will be borrowed than can be lent, for the plow represents here the total of available capital.

True, I have reduced the operation to its simplest terms; but test by the same touchstone the most complicated governmental credit institutions, and you will be convinced that they can have but one result: to reallocate credit, not to *increase* it. In a given country and at a given time, there is only a certain sum of available capital, and it is all placed somewhere. By guaranteeing insolvent debtors, the state can certainly increase the number of borrowers, raise the rate of interest (all at the expense of the taxpayer), but it cannot increase the number of lenders and the total value of the loans.

Do not impute to me, however, a conclusion from which I beg Heaven to preserve me. I say that the law should not artificially encourage borrowing; but I do not say that it should hinder it artificially. If in our hypothetical system or elsewhere there should be obstacles to the diffusion and application of credit, let the law remove them; nothing could be better or more just. But that, along with liberty, is all that social reformers worthy of the name should ask of the law.[7]

---

[7]. [See the end of the twelfth letter on *Interest-free Credit*, Vol, V, pages 282 ff. (of the French edition).—Editor.]

Step 3

Hands-On Activity 1

Experiential Learning

Draw two BOT graphs showing what happens when the credit market operates freely and when the government guarantees loans of unworthy borrowers. In addition, draw one CLD of Bastiat's description of "what is seen" and "what is not seen" in the economy when loan repayments are guaranteed by government.

Hands-On Activity 2

Experiential Learning

Find a news article about TARP (Troubled Assets Relief Program) and draw BOT graphs and CLDs of "what is seen" and "what is not seen" in the economy as a result of TARP.

Activity 1 BOT: Credit

Free Market for Credit	Unworthy Borrower Loans Guaranteed by Government

Unit 9: *Credit*

Activity 1 CLD

Activity 2 BOT

Activity 2 CLD

Step 4

Journal Writing

<u>Reflection and Synthesis</u>
Record in a journal your reactions to the learning.

Unit 9: Credit

Step 5
Evaluation Notes

Evaluation
Compare "what you saw" (your presumptions) with "what you did not see" (what you learned).

What I saw	What I did not see
1. I first saw..... .	1. But what I did not see was...

Unit 10: Algeria

> ### Step 1
>
> ## Free Writing
>
> <u>Culturally-based presumptions</u>
> Write what you think happens in the economy when a government uses taxes for a colonization program where its citizens receive transport, housing, and employment subsidies.

Unit 10: Algeria

Step 2

Information Gap Writing

<u>New knowledge</u>
Read "Algeria." Compare your presumptions with what is learned.

Presumptions	New Knowledge	Information Gaps

107

Algeria

Four orators are all trying to be heard in the Assembly. At first they speak all at once, then one after the other. What have they said? Very beautiful things, surely, about the power and grandeur of France, the necessity of sowing in order to reap, the brilliant future of our vast colony, the advantage of redistributing our *surplus* population, etc., etc.; masterpieces of eloquence, always ornamented with this conclusion:

"Vote fifty million francs (more or less) to build ports and roads in Algeria so that we can transport colonists there, build houses for them, and clear fields for them. If you do this, you will have lifted a burden from the shoulders of the French worker, encouraged employment in Africa, and increased trade in Marseilles. It would be all profit."

Yes, that is true, if we consider the said fifty million francs only from the moment when the state spends them, if we look at where they go, and not whence they come, if we take into account only the good that they will do after they leave the coffers of the tax collectors, and not the harm that has been brought about, or, beyond that, the good that has been prevented, by causing them to enter the government coffers in the first place. Yes, from this limited point of view, everything is profit. The house built in Barbary is *what is seen;* the port laid out in Barbary is *what is seen;* the jobs created in Barbary are what *is seen;* a certain reduction in the labor force in France is *what is seen;* great business activity in Marseilles, *still what is seen.*

But there is something else *that is not seen*. It is that the fifty millions spent by the state can no longer be spent as they would have been by the taxpayers. From all the benefits attributed to public spending we must deduct all the harm caused by preventing private spending—at least if we are not to go so far as to say that James Goodfellow would have done nothing with the five-franc pieces he had fairly earned and that the tax took away from him; an absurd assertion, for if he went to the trouble of earning them, it was because he hoped to have the satisfaction of using them. He would have had his garden fenced and can no longer do so; *this is what is not seen*. He would have had his field marled and can no longer do so: *this is what is not seen*. He would have added to his tools and can no longer do so: *this is what is not seen*. He would be better fed, better clothed; he would have had his sons better educated; he would have increased the dowry of his daughter, and he can no longer do so: *this is what is not seen*. He would have joined a mutual-aid society and can no longer do so: *this is what is not seen*. On the one hand, the satisfactions that have been taken away from him and the means of action that have been destroyed in his hands; on the other hand, the work of the ditchdigger, the carpenter, the blacksmith, the tailor, and the schoolmaster of his village which he would have encouraged and which is now nonexistent: *this is still what is not seen.*

Our citizens are counting a great deal on the future prosperity of Algeria; granted. But let them also calculate the paralysis that in the meantime will inevitably strike France. People show me business flourishing in Marseilles; but if it is transacted with the product of taxation, I shall, on the other hand, point out an equal amount of business destroyed in the rest of the country. They say: "A colonist transported to Barbary is relief for the population that remains in the country." I reply: "How can that be if, in transporting this colonist to Algeria, we have also transported two or three times the capital that would have kept him alive in France?"[8]

The only end I have in view is to make the reader understand that, in all public spending, behind the apparent good there is an evil more difficult to discern. To the best of my ability, I should like to get my reader into the habit of seeing the one and the other and of taking account of both.

When a public expenditure is proposed, it must be examined on its own merits, apart from its allegedly beneficial effect in increasing the number of jobs available, for any improvement in this direction is illusory. What public spending does in this regard, private spending would have done to the same extent. Therefore, the employment issue is irrelevant.

It is not within the province of this essay to evaluate the intrinsic worth of the public expenditures devoted to Algeria.

But I cannot refrain from making one general observation. It is that a presumption of economic benefit is never appropriate for expenditures made by way of taxation. Why? Here is the reason.

In the first place, justice always suffers from it somewhat. Since James Goodfellow has sweated to earn his hundred-sou piece with some satisfaction in view, he is irritated, to say the least, that the tax intervenes to take this satisfaction away from him and give it to someone else.

Now, certainly it is up to those who levy the tax to give some good reasons for it. We have seen that the state gives a detestable reason when it says: "With these hundred sous I am going to put some men to work," for James Goodfellow (as soon as he has seen the light) will not fail to respond: "Good Lord! With a hundred sous I could have put them to work myself."

Once this argument on the part of the state has been disposed of, the others present themselves in all their nakedness, and the debate between the public treasury and poor James is very much simplified. If the state says to him: "I shall take a hundred sous from you to pay the policemen who relieve you of the necessity for guarding your own security, to pave the street you traverse every day, to pay the magistrate who sees to it that your property and your liberty are respected, to feed the soldier who defends our frontiers," James Goodfellow will pay without saying a word, or I am greatly mistaken. But if the state says to him: "I shall take your hundred sous to give you one sou as a premium in case you have cultivated your field well, or to teach your son what you do not want him to learn, or to allow a cabinet minister to add a hundred-and-first dish to his dinner; I shall take them to build a cottage in Algeria, not to mention taking a hundred sous more to support a colonist there and another hundred sous to support a soldier to guard the colonist and another hundred sous to support a general to watch over the soldier, etc., etc.," it seems to me that I hear poor James cry out: "This legal system very strongly resembles the law of the jungle!" And as the state foresees the objection, what does it do? It confuses everything; it advances a detestable argument that ought not to have any influence on the question: it speaks of the effect of the hundred sous on employment; it points to the cook and to the tradesman who supplies the needs of the minister; it shows us a colonist, a soldier, a general, living on the five francs; it shows us, in short, *what is seen*. As long as James Goodfellow has not learned to put next to this *what is not seen,* he will be duped. That is why I am forced to teach him by loud and long repetition.

From the fact that public expenditures reallocate jobs without increasing them there results against such expenditures a second and grave objection. To reallocate jobs is to displace workers and to disturb the natural laws that govern the distribution of population over the earth. When fifty million francs are left to the taxpayers, since the latter are situated throughout the country, the money fosters employment in the forty thousand municipalities of France; it acts as a bond that holds each man to his native land; it is distributed to as many workers as possible and to all imaginable industries. Now, if the state, taking these fifty millions from the citizens, accumulates them and spends them at a given place, it will draw to this place a proportional quantity of labor it has transferred from other places, a corresponding number of expatriated workers, a floating population, declassed, and, I daresay, dangerous when the money is used up! But this is what happens (and here I return to my subject): this feverish activity, blown, so to speak, into a narrow space, attracts everyone's eye and is *what is seen;* the people applaud, marvel at the beauty and ease of the procedure, and demand its repetition and extension. *What is not seen* is that an equal number of jobs, probably more useful, have been prevented from being created in the rest of France.

---

[8] The Honorable Minister of War has recently affirmed that each individual transported to Algeria has cost the state eight thousand francs. Now, it is certain that the poor people involved could have lived very well in France on a capital of four thousand francs. How, I should like to know, do you help the French people when you take away one man and the means of existence for two?

Step 3

Hands-On Activity 1

Experiential Learning

Draw two BOT graphs and one CLD of Bastiat's description of "what is seen" and "what is not seen" in the economy when the French government provides fifty million francs to transport, house, and clear fields for its colonists.

Hands-On Activity 2

Experiential Learning

Find a news article about a government housing program and draw BOT graphs and CLDs of "what is seen" and "what is not seen" in the economy as a result of the housing program.

Activity 1 BOT: Algeria

What Is Seen	What Is NOT Seen

Activity 1 CLD

Activity 2 BOT

Activity 2 CLD

Step 4

Journal Writing

Reflection and Synthesis
Record in a journal your reactions to the learning.

Unit 10: Algeria

Step 5

Evaluation Notes

<u>Evaluation</u>
Compare "what you saw" (your presumptions) with "what you did not see" (what you learned).

What I saw	What I did not see
1. I first saw….. .	1. But what I did not see was…

Unit 11: Thrift and Luxury

Step 1

Free Writing

<u>Culturally-based presumptions</u>

Write what you think happens in the economy when two brothers, Ariste and Mondor, both receive $5 million of inheritance and Mondor spends his money on luxuries whereas Ariste spends his money on his and his family's needs.

Unit 11: Thrift and Luxury

Step 2

Information Gap Writing

<u>New knowledge</u>
Read "Thrift and Luxury." Compare your presumptions with what is learned.

Presumptions	New Knowledge	Information Gaps

117

Thrift and Luxury

It is not only in the matter of public expenditures that *what is seen* eclipses *what is not seen*. By leaving in the shadow half of the political economy, this phenomenon of the seen and the unseen induces a false moral standard. It leads nations to view their moral interests and their material interests as antagonistic. What could be more discouraging or more tragic? Observe:

There is no father of a family who does not take it as his duty to teach his children order, good management, economy, thrift, moderation in spending.

There is no religion that does not inveigh against ostentation and luxury. That is all well and good; but, on the other hand, what is more popular than these adages:

"To hoard is to dry up the veins of the people."

"The luxury of the great makes for the comfort of the little fellow."

"Prodigals ruin themselves, but they enrich the state."

"It is with the surplus of the rich that the bread of the poor is made."

Certainly there is a flagrant contradiction here between the moral idea and the economic idea. How many eminent men, after having pointed out this conflict, look upon it with equanimity! This is what I have never been able to understand; for it seems to me that one can experience nothing more painful than to see two opposing tendencies in the heart of man. Mankind will be degraded by the one extreme as well as by the other! If thrifty, it will fall into dire want; if prodigal, it will fall into moral bankruptcy!

Fortunately, these popular maxims represent thrift and luxury in a false light, taking account only of the immediate consequences *that are seen* and not of the more remote effects *that are not seen*. Let us try to rectify this incomplete view.

Mondor and his brother Ariste, having divided their paternal inheritance, each have an income of fifty thousand francs a year. Mondor practices philanthropy in the fashionable way. He is a spendthrift. He replaces his furniture several times a year, changes his carriages every month; people talk about the ingenious devices to which he resorts to get rid of his money faster; in brief, he makes the high livers of Balzac and Alexander Dumas look pale by comparison.

What a chorus of praises always surround him! "Tell us about Mondor! Long live Mondor! He is the benefactor of the workingman. He is the good angel of the people! It is true that he wallows in luxury; he splashes pedestrians with mud; his own dignity and human dignity in general suffer somewhat from it. .... But what of it? If he does not make himself useful by his own labor, he does so by means of his wealth. He puts money into circulation. His courtyard is never empty of tradesmen who always leave satisfied. Don't people say that coins are round so that they can roll?"

Ariste has adopted a quite different plan of life. If he is not an egoist, he is at least an *individualist;* for he is rational in his spending, seeks only moderate and reasonable enjoyments, thinks of the future of his children; in a word, he *saves.*

And now I want you to hear what the crowd says about him!

"What good is this mean rich man, this penny-pincher? Undoubtedly there is something impressive and touching in the simplicity of his life; furthermore, he is humane, benevolent, and generous. But he *calculates.* He does not run through his whole income. His house is not always shining with lights and swarming with people. What gratitude do the carpetmakers, the coachmakers, the horse dealers, and the confectioners owe to him?"

These judgments, disastrous to morality, are founded on the fact that there is one thing that strikes the eye: the spending of the prodigal brother; and another thing that escapes the eye: the equal or even greater spending of the economical brother.

But things have been so admirably arranged by the divine Inventor of the social order that in this, as in everything, political economy and morality, far from clashing, are in harmony, so that the wisdom of Ariste is not only more worthy, but even more *profitable,* than the folly of Mondor.

And when I say more profitable, I do not mean only more profitable to Ariste, or even to society in general, but more profitable to present-day workers, to the industry of the age.

To prove this, it suffices to set before the mind's eye those hidden consequences of human actions that the bodily eye does not see.

Yes, the prodigality of Mondor has effects visible to all eyes: everyone can see his berlines, his landaus, his phaetons, the delicate paintings on his ceilings, his rich carpets, the splendor of his mansion. Everyone knows that he runs his thoroughbreds in the races. The dinners that he gives at his mansion in Paris fascinate the crowd on the boulevard, and people say to one another: "There's a fine fellow, who, far from saving any of his income, is probably making a hole in his capital." *This is what is seen.*

It is not as easy to see, from the viewpoint of the interest of the workers, what becomes of Ariste's income. If we trace it, however, we shall assure ourselves that all of it, *down to the last centime*, goes to give employment to the workers, just as certainly as the income of Mondor. There is only this difference: The foolish spending of Mondor is bound to decrease continually and to reach a necessary end; the wise spending of Ariste will go on increasing year by year.

And if this is the case, certainly the public interest is in accord with morality.

Ariste spends for himself and his house twenty thousand francs a year. If this does not suffice to make him happy, he does not deserve to be called wise. He is touched by the ills that weigh on the poor; he feels morally obligated to relieve them somewhat and devotes ten thousand francs to acts of charity. Among businessmen, manufacturers, and farmers he has friends who, for the moment, find themselves financially embarrassed. He inquires about their situation in order to come to their aid prudently and efficaciously and sets aside for this work another ten thousand francs. Finally, he does not forget that he has daughters to provide dowries for, sons to assure a future for, and, consequently, he imposes on himself the duty of saving and investing ten thousand francs a year.

This, then, is how he uses his income:

1. Personal expenses . . . . . 20,000 francs

2. Charity . . . . 10,000 francs

3. Help to friends . . . . 10,000 francs

4. Savings . . . . 10,000 francs

If we review each of these items, we shall see that not a centime escapes going into the support of national industry.

1. *Personal expenses.* These, for workmen and shopkeepers, have effects absolutely identical to an equal amount spent by Mondor. This is self-evident; let us not discuss it further.
2. *Charity.* The ten thousand francs devoted to this end will support industry just as much; they will go to the baker, the butcher, the tailor, and the furniture dealer, except that the bread, the meat, the clothes do not serve the needs of Ariste directly, but of those whom he has substituted for himself. Now, this simple substitution of one consumer for another has no effect at all on industry in general. Whether Ariste spends a hundred sous or asks a poor person to spend it in his place is all one.
3. *Help to friends.* The friend to whom Ariste lends or gives ten thousand francs does not receive them in order to bury them; that would be contrary to our hypothesis. He uses them to pay for merchandise or to pay off his debts. In the first case, industry is encouraged. Will anyone dare say that there is more gained from Mondor's purchase of a thoroughbred for ten thousand francs than from a purchase by Ariste or his friends of ten thousand francs' worth of cloth? If this sum serves to pay a debt, all that results is that a third person appears, the creditor, who will handle the ten thousand francs, but who will certainly use them for something in his business, his factory, or his exploitation of natural resources. He is just one more intermediary between Ariste and the workers. The names change, the spending remains, and so does the encouragement of industry.
4. *Savings.* There remain the ten thousand francs *saved;* and it is here that, from the point of view of encouragement of the arts, industry, and the employment of workers, Mondor appears superior to Ariste, although morally Ariste shows himself a little superior to Mondor.

It is not without actual physical pain that I see such contradictions appear between the great laws of Nature. If mankind were reduced to choosing between the two sides, one of which hurts its interests and the other its conscience, we should have to despair for its future. Happily this is not so.[9] To see Ariste regain his economic as well as his moral superiority, we need only understand this consoling axiom, which is not the less true for having a paradoxical appearance: *To save is to spend.*

What is Ariste's object in saving ten thousand francs? Is it to hide two thousand hundred-sou pieces in a hole in his garden? No, certainly not. He intends to increase his capital and his income. Consequently, this money that he does not use to buy personal satisfactions he uses to buy pieces of land, a house, government bonds, industrial enterprises; or perhaps he invests it with a broker or a banker. Follow the money through all these hypothetical uses, and you will be convinced that, through the intermediary of sellers or borrowers, it will go to support industry just as surely as if Ariste, following the example of his brother, had exchanged it for furniture, jewels, and horses.

For when Ariste buys for ten thousand francs pieces of land or bonds, he does so because he feels he does not need to spend this sum. This seems to be what you hold against him.

But, by the same token, the person who sells the piece of land or the mortgage is going to have to spend in some way the ten thousand francs he receives.

So that the spending is done in either case, whether by Ariste or by those who are substituted for him.

From the point of view of the working class and of the support given to industry, there is, then, only one difference between the conduct of Ariste and that of Mondor. The spending of Mondor is directly accomplished by him and around him; *it is seen.* That of Ariste, being carried out partly by intermediaries and at a distance, *is not seen.* But in fact, for anyone who can connect effects to their causes, that which is not seen is every bit as real as that which is seen. What proves it is that in both cases the money *circulates,* and that no more of it remains in the coffers of the wise brother than in those of the prodigal.

It is therefore false to say that thrift does actual harm to industry. In this respect it is just as beneficial as luxury.

But how superior it appears, if our thinking, instead of confining itself to the passing hour, embraces a long period of time!

Ten years have gone by. What has become of Mondor and his fortune and his great popularity? It has all vanished. Mondor is ruined; far from pouring fifty thousands francs into the economy every year, he is probably a public charge. In any case he is no longer the joy of the shopkeepers; he is no longer considered a promoter of the arts and of industry; he is no longer any good to the workers, nor to his descendants, whom he leaves in distress.

At the end of the same ten years Ariste not only continues to put all of his income into circulation, but he contributes increasing income from year to year. He adds to the national capital, that is to say, the funds that provide wages; and since the demand for workers depends on the extent of these funds, he contributes to the progressive increase of remuneration of the working class. Should he die, he will leave children who will replace him in this work of progress and civilization.

Morally, the superiority of thrift over luxury is incontestable. It is consoling to think that, from the economic point of view, it has the same superiority for whoever, not stopping at the immediate effects of things, can push his investigations to their ultimate effects.

---

[9] [See note 5 *supra*.—Editor.]

> # Step 3
>
> ## Hands-On Activity 1
>
> <u>Experiential Learning</u>
> Draw BOT graphs and CLDs for the brothers Ariste and Mondor using Bastiat's description of "what is seen" and "what is not seen" in the economy as a result of their spending habits.
>
> ## Hands-On Activity 2
>
> <u>Experiential Learning</u>
> Find a news article about spending and savings and draw separate BOT graphs and CLDs of "what is seen" and "what is not seen" in the economy for both spending and savings.

Activity 1 BOT *What Is Seen* **Mondor**	*What Is NOT Seen* **Mondor**
Ariste	**Ariste**

Unit 11: Thrift and Luxury

Activity 1 CLD
Mondor

Ariste

Activity 2 BOT

Activity 2 CLD

Step 4

Journal Writing

Reflection and Synthesis
Record in a journal your reactions to the learning.

Unit 11: Thrift and Luxury

Step 5

Evaluation Notes

<u>Evaluation</u>
Compare "what you saw" (your presumptions) with "what you did not see" (what you learned).

What I saw	What I did not see
1. I first saw..... .	1. But what I did not see was…

Unit 12: Right to Employment and Profit

Step 1

Free Writing

Culturally-based presumptions

Write what you think happens in the economy when a government creates a "jobs" program and pays people from the tax dollars a set salary or wage for an indefinite amount of time.

Unit 12: Right to Employment and Profit

Step 2

Information Gap Writing

<u>New knowledge</u>
Read "The Right to Employment and the Right to Profit." Compare your presumptions with what is learned.

Presumptions	New Knowledge	Information Gaps

The Right to Employment and the Right to Profit

"Brothers, assess yourselves to furnish me work at your price." This is the right to employment, elementary or first-degree socialism.

"Brothers, assess yourselves to furnish me work at my price." This is the right to profit, refined or second-degree socialism.

Both live by virtue of such of their effects *as are seen*. They will die from those of their effects *that are not seen*.

What is seen is the work and the profit stimulated by the assessments levied on society. *What is not seen* is the work and the profits that would come from this same amount of money if it were left in the hands of the taxpayers themselves.

In 1848 the right to employment showed itself for a moment with two faces. That was enough to ruin it in public opinion.

One of these faces was called: *National workshop*.

The other: *Forty-five centimes*.*

Millions went every day from the rue de Rivoli to the national workshops. This was the beautiful side of the coin.

But here is what was on the other side. In order for millions of francs to come out of a coffer, they must first have come into it. That is why the organizers of the right to employment addressed themselves to the taxpayers.

---

* [The new regime brought in by the February Revolution sponsored national workshops to deal with the unemployment problem and also added forty-five centimes to the rate of indirect taxation. The workshops proved to be an unsatisfactory solution of the unemployment problem, a farcical system of handouts for little or no work. When it was decided to abolish the national workshops and find the unemployed places in the army, public works, or private industry, the workingmen of Paris, incensed at the government's betrayal of the "right to employment," revolted and were subdued, after fierce fighting, in June, 1849.—Translator.]

Unit 12: Right to Employment and Profit

Now, the farmers said: "I must pay forty-five centimes. Then I shall be deprived of clothes; I cannot marl my field; I cannot have my house repaired."

And the hired hands said: "Since our boss is not going to have any new clothes, there will be less work for the tailor; since he is not going to have his field marled, there will be less work for the ditchdigger; since he is not going to have his house repaired, there will be less work for the carpenter and the mason."

It was therefore proved that you cannot profit twice from the same transaction, and that the work paid for by the government was created at the expense of work that would have been paid for by the taxpayer. That was the end of the right to employment, which came to be seen as an illusion as well as an injustice.

However, the right to profit, which is nothing but an exaggeration of the right to employment, is still alive and flourishing.

Is there not something shameful in the role that the protectionist makes society play?

He says to society:

"You must give me work, and, what is more, lucrative work. I have foolishly chosen an industry that leaves me with a loss of ten per cent. If you slap a tax of twenty francs on my fellow citizens and excuse me from paying it, my loss will be converted into a profit. Now, profit is a right; you owe it to me."

The society that listens to this sophist, that will levy taxes on itself to satisfy him, that does not perceive that the loss wiped out in one industry is no less a loss because others are forced to shoulder it—this society, I say, deserves the burden placed upon it.

Thus, we see, from the many subjects I have dealt with, that not to know political economy is to allow oneself to be dazzled by the immediate effect of a phenomenon; to know political economy is to take into account the sum total of all effects, both immediate and future.[10]

I could submit here a host of other questions to the same test. But I desist from doing so, because of the monotony of demonstrations that would always be the same, and I conclude by applying to political economy what Chateaubriand† said of history:

There are two consequences in history: one immediate and instantaneously recognized; the other distant and unperceived at first. These consequences often contradict each other; the former come from our short-run wisdom, the latter from long-run wisdom. The providential event appears after the human event. Behind men rises God. Deny as much as you wish the Supreme Wisdom, do not believe in its action, dispute over words, call what the common man calls Providence "the force of circumstances" or "reason"; but look at the end of an accomplished fact, and you will see that it has always produced the opposite of what was expected when it has not been founded from the first on morality and justice.

(Chateaubriand, *Memoirs from beyond the Tomb*.)

---

10 If all the consequences of an action redounded on its author, we should soon enough receive our education. But this is not the case. Sometimes the visible good effects are for us, and the invisible bad effects are for others, which makes them all the more invisible. We must therefore wait for the reaction to come from those who have to endure the bad consequences of the act. Occasionally this takes a long time, and that is what prolongs the reign of error.

A man does something that produces good effects equal to ten, to his profit, and bad effects equal to fifteen, divided among thirty of his fellows in such a way that each of them receives only one half. In the total there is a loss, and there must necessarily be a reaction. We must concede, however, that it will be all the longer in coming because the bad effects are spread out so widely among the masses, while the good are concentrated at one point. [Unpublished fragment of the author.]

---

† [Vicomte François René de Chateaubriand (1768–1848), a forerunner of the romantic movement in French literature, and a royalist of the Bourbon stamp in politics. He served the restored Bourbon monarchy, after Napoleon's fall, as ambassador to England and Germany and as Minister of Foreign Affairs. His most famous works were *The Genius of Christianity* and *Memoirs from beyond the Tomb*.—Translator.]

Step 3

Hands-On Activity 1

<u>Experiential Learning</u>
Draw BOT graphs and one CLD for Bastiat's description of "what is seen" and "what is not seen" in the economy with "The Right to Employment and the Right to Profit" program.

Hands-On Activity 2

<u>Experiential Learning</u>
Find a news article about a national jobs program, such as the 2010 US jobs program, and draw a BOT graph and CLDs of "what is seen" and "what is not seen" in the economy as a result the program.

Activity 1 BOT: Right to Employment and Profit	
What Is Seen National Works Program	*What Is NOT Seen* National Works Program
Right to Profit Program	Right to Profit Program

Activity 1 CLD

Activity 2 BOT

Unit 12: Right to Employment and Profit

Activity 2 CLD

Step 4

Journal Writing

<u>Reflection and Synthesis</u>
Record in a journal your reactions to the learning.

Step 5

Evaluation Notes

<u>Evaluation</u>
Compare "what you saw" (your presumptions) with "what you did not see" (what you learned).

What I saw	What I did not see
1. I first saw….. .	1. But what I did not see was…

Appendix
Learning Activities and Suggested Responses

Important Note:

"What Is NOT Seen" lines and loops are dotted lines.

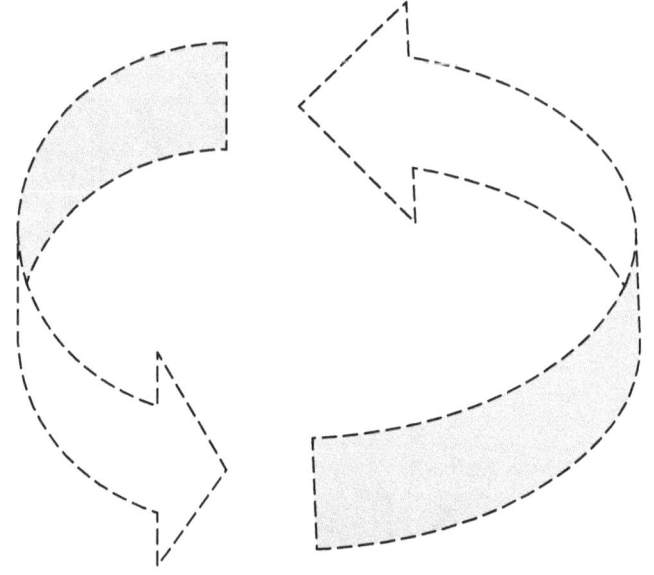

Hands-On Activity 1, Unit 1: The Broken Window

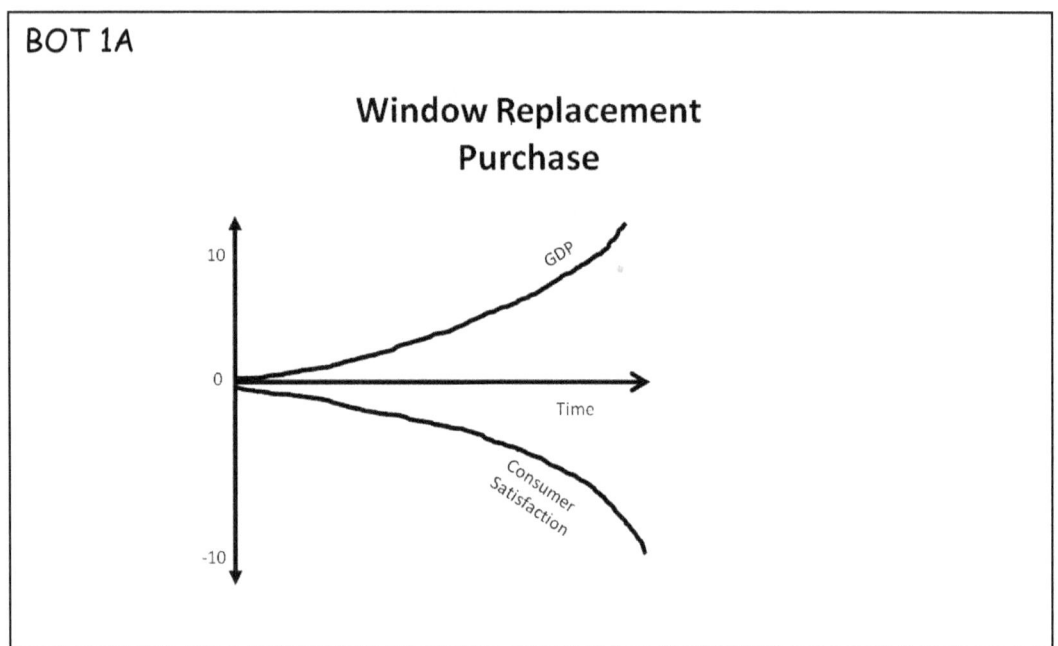

"No Net Satisfaction from Broken Window."
"Society Loses Value of Window."

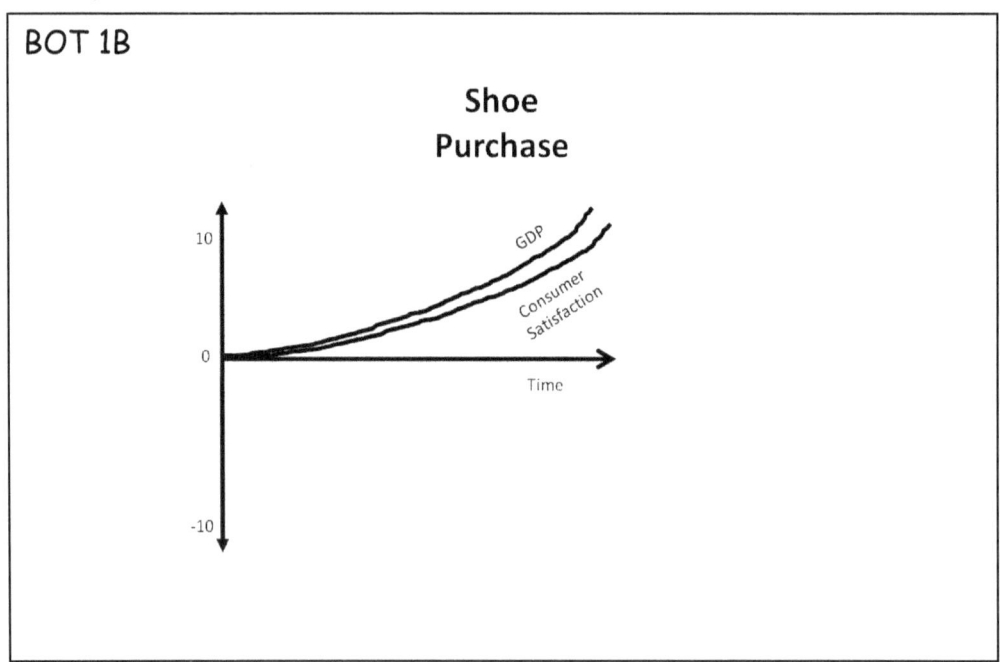

"Increase in Satisfaction."
"Consumer Enjoys Both Window and Shoes."

Appendix: Learning Activities and Suggested Responses

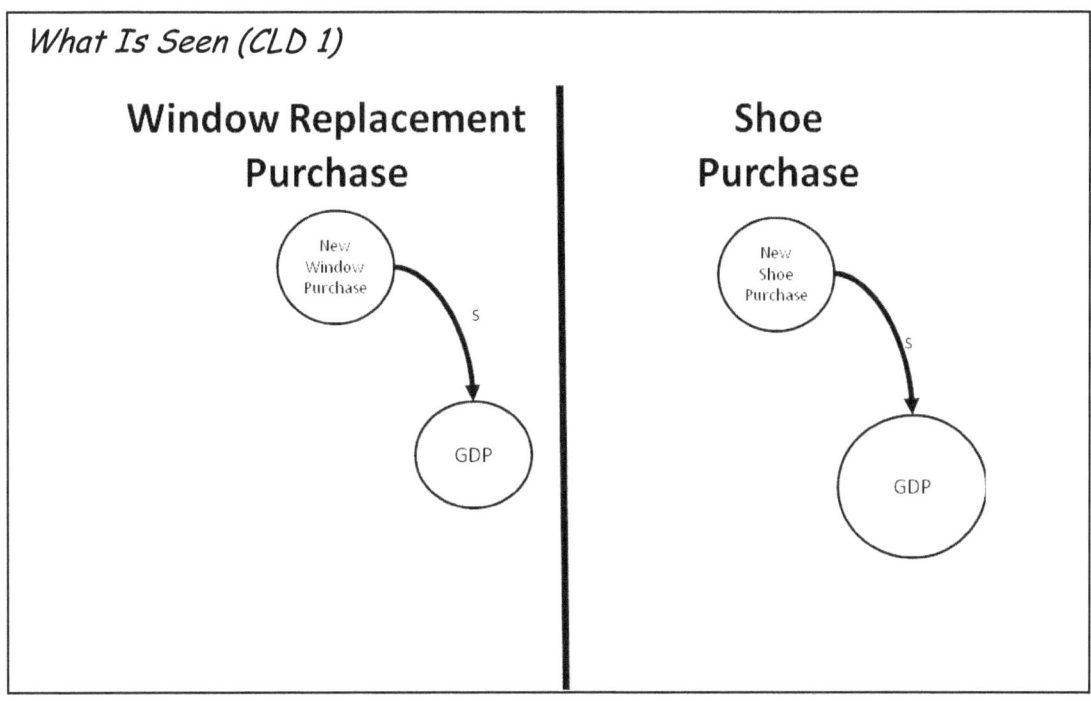

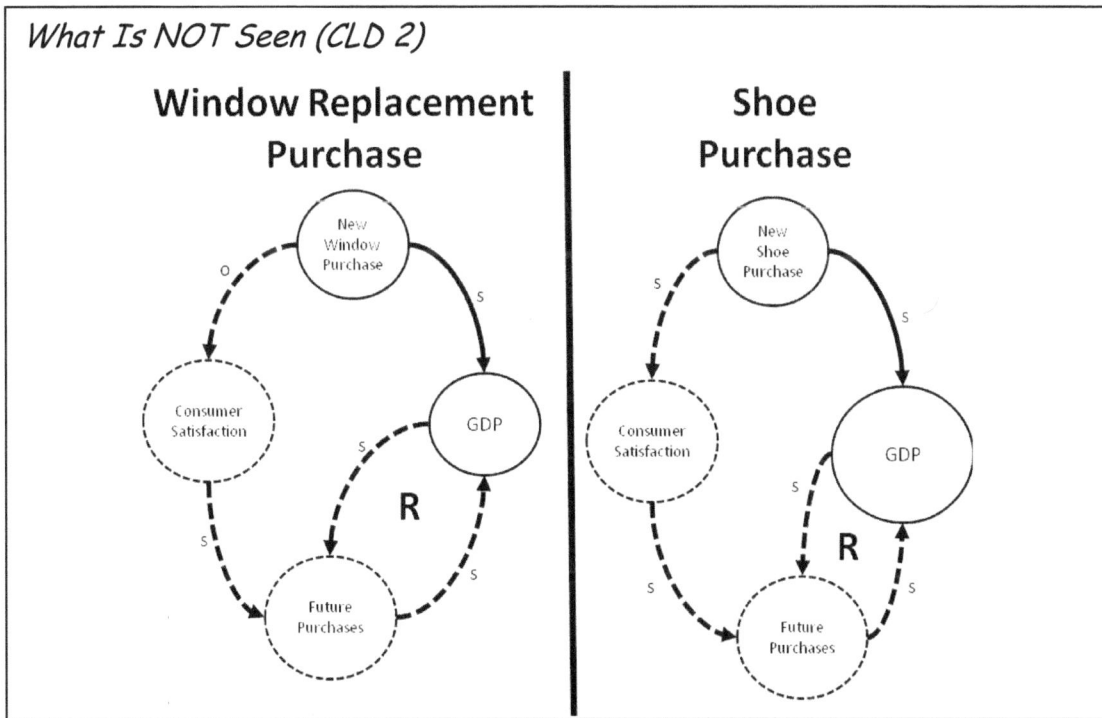

Window replacement purchase actually decreases GDP, whereas the satisfaction the consumer gets from purchasing new shoes causes him or her to make future purchases; thus increasing GDP in the long-term.

Hands-On Activity 1, Unit 2: The Demobilization

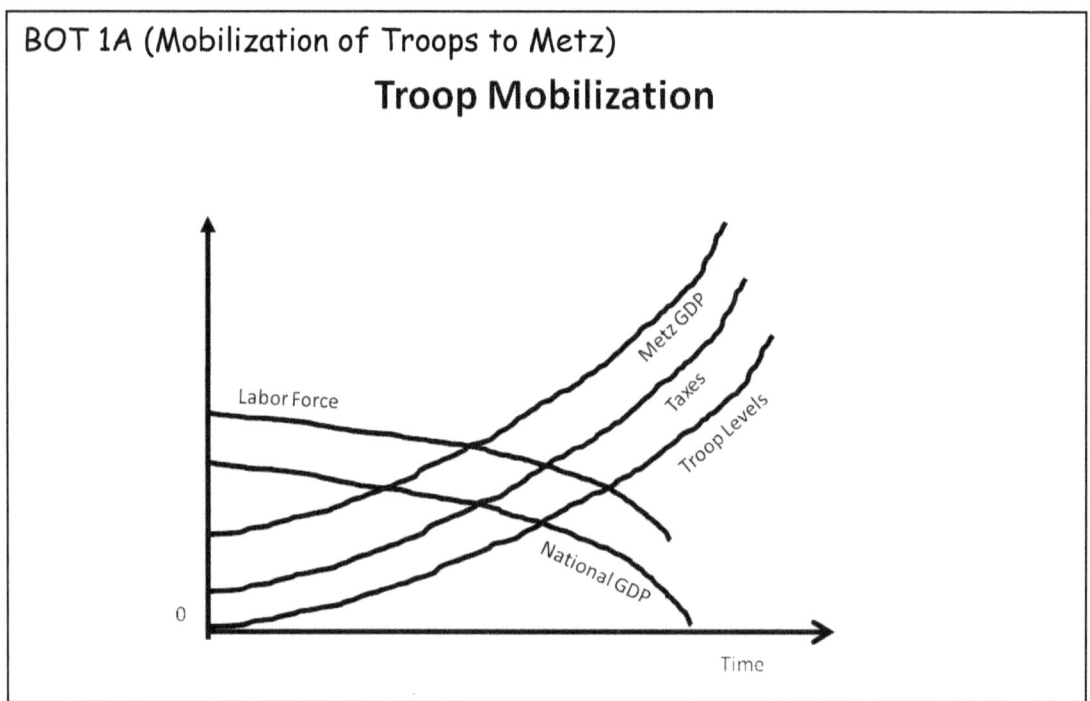

Because of an increase in taxes, a reduction in the national labor pool, and a decline in material production, the national GDP suffers.

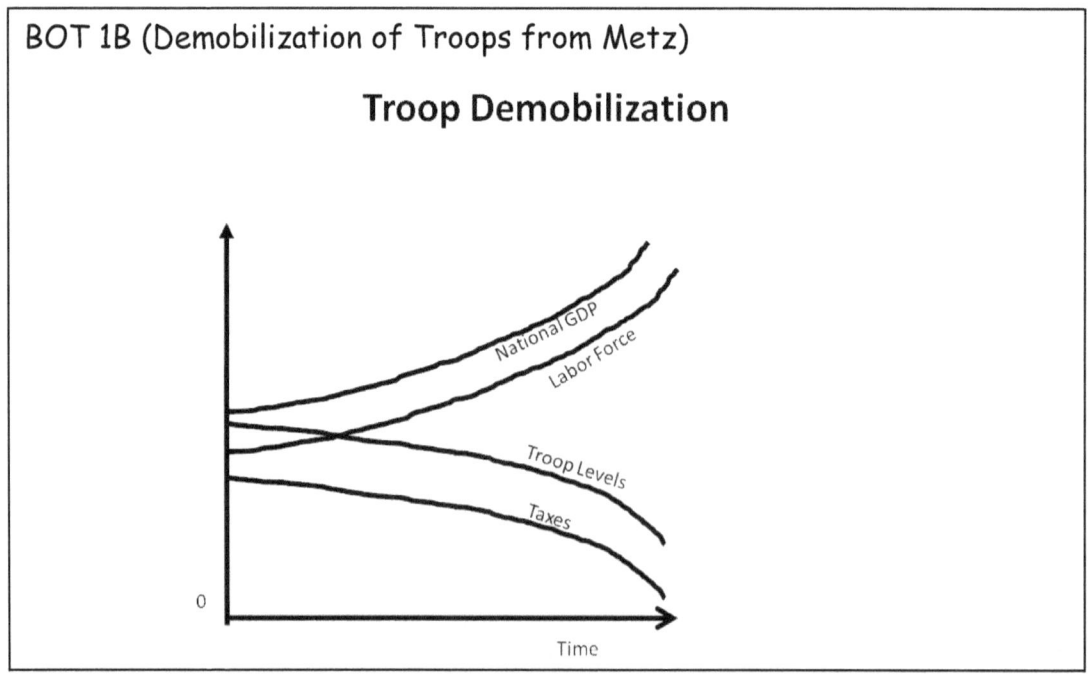

Demobilization decreases taxes and increases the labor force; thus increasing material production and national GDP.

Appendix: Learning Activities and Suggested Responses

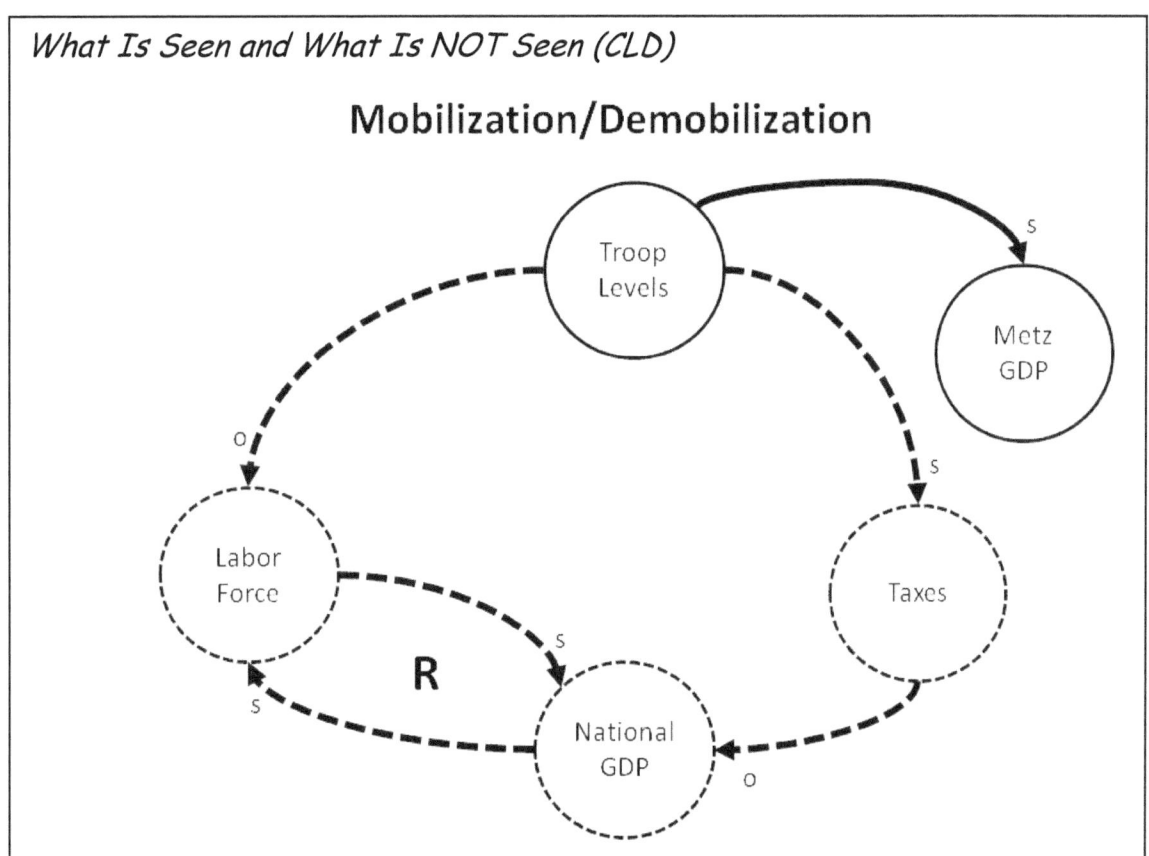

Even though the Metz GDP increases, mobilization causes an increase in taxes which causes a decline in national GDP which in turn causes a decline in the labor force which causes a further decline in national GDP. Furthermore, mobilization causes a decline in the labor force because some persons must move out of the natural economy into a military barracks in Metz and this also causes a decline in national GDP. On the other hand, demobilization causes the national GDP to increase even though the Metz GDP declines because taxes will not be assessed for supporting troops and the government will not have tampered with the labor pool.

Hands-On Activity 1, Unit 3: Taxes

What Is Seen

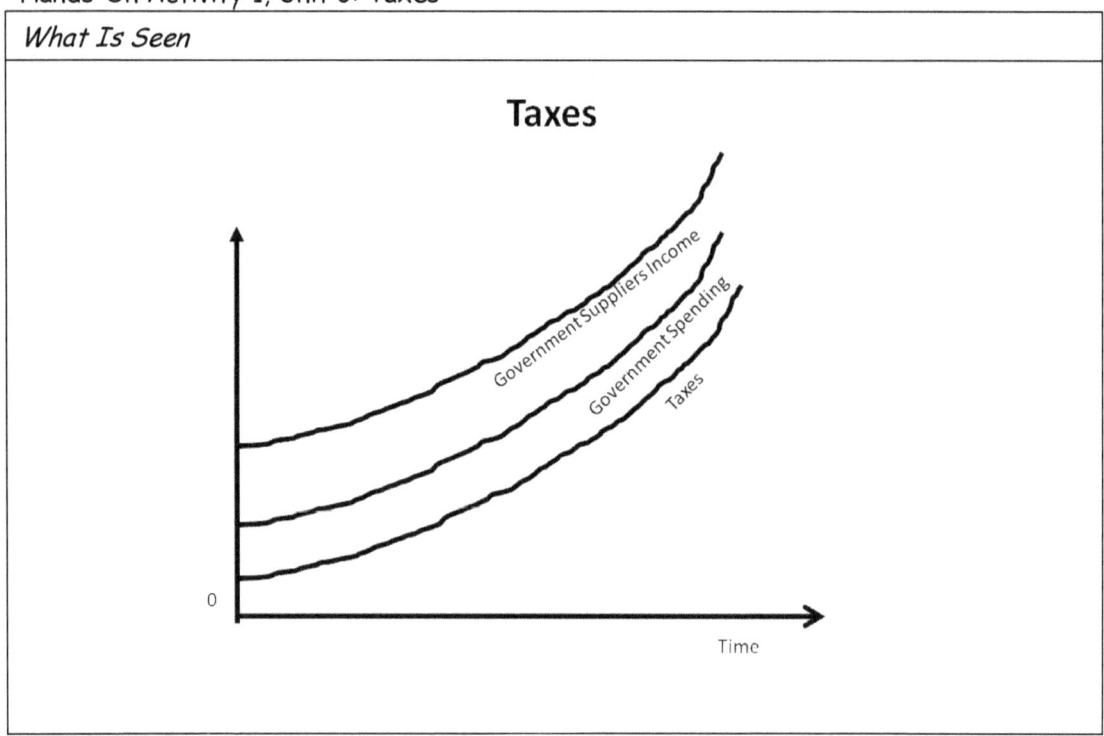

People see that government spending increases income for government suppliers.

What Is NOT Seen

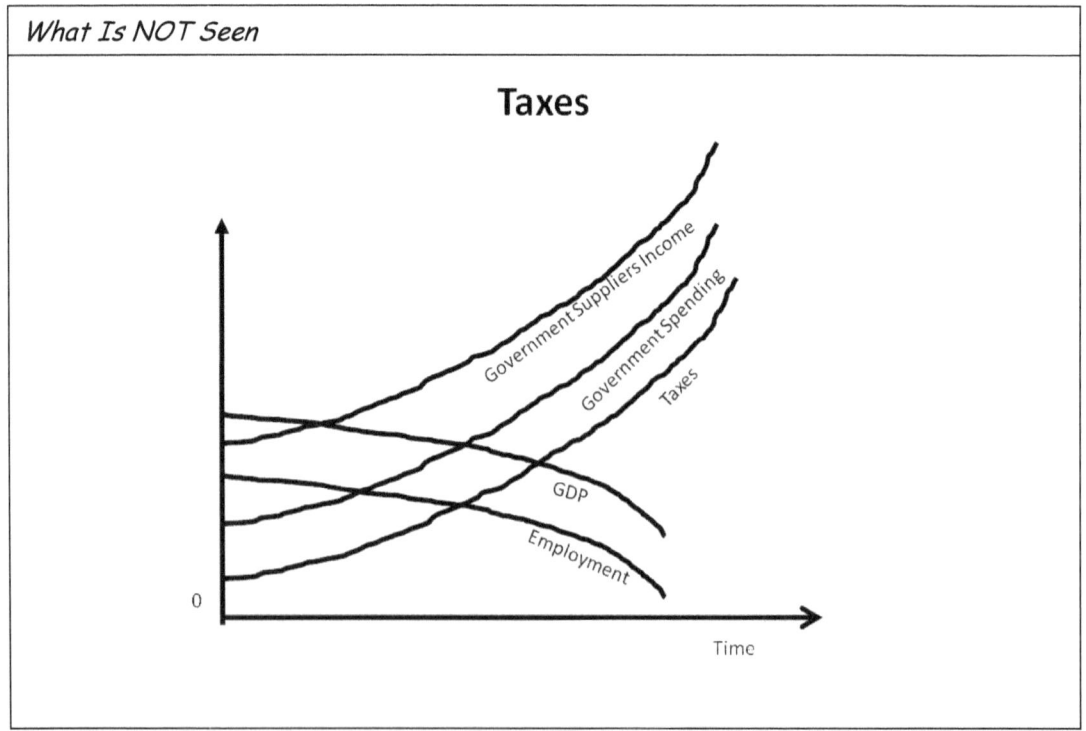

People do not see that government spending decreases GDP and employment.

Appendix: Learning Activities and Suggested Responses

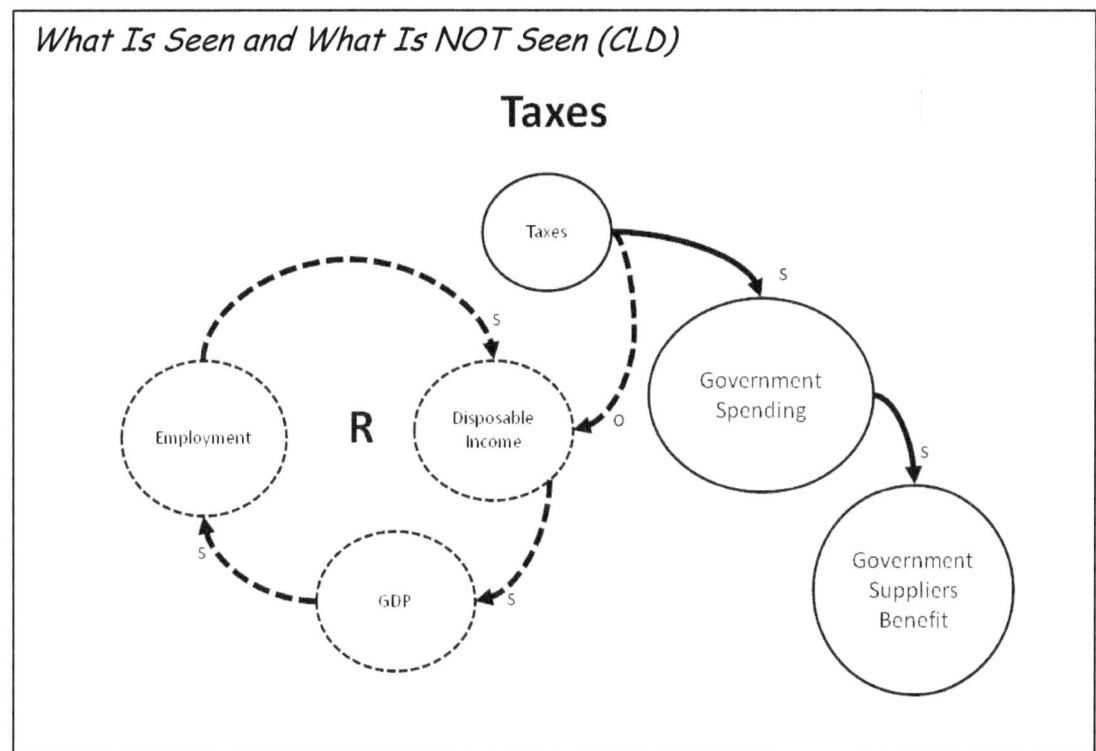

People see that taxes go towards government spending which in turn benefits government suppliers. However, what people do not see is that taxes decrease disposable income which in turn decreases GDP which in turn decreases employment and this then causes further declines in disposable income and GDP.

Hands-On Activity 1, Unit 4: Theaters and Fine Arts

What Is Seen

Theaters and Fine Arts Subsidies

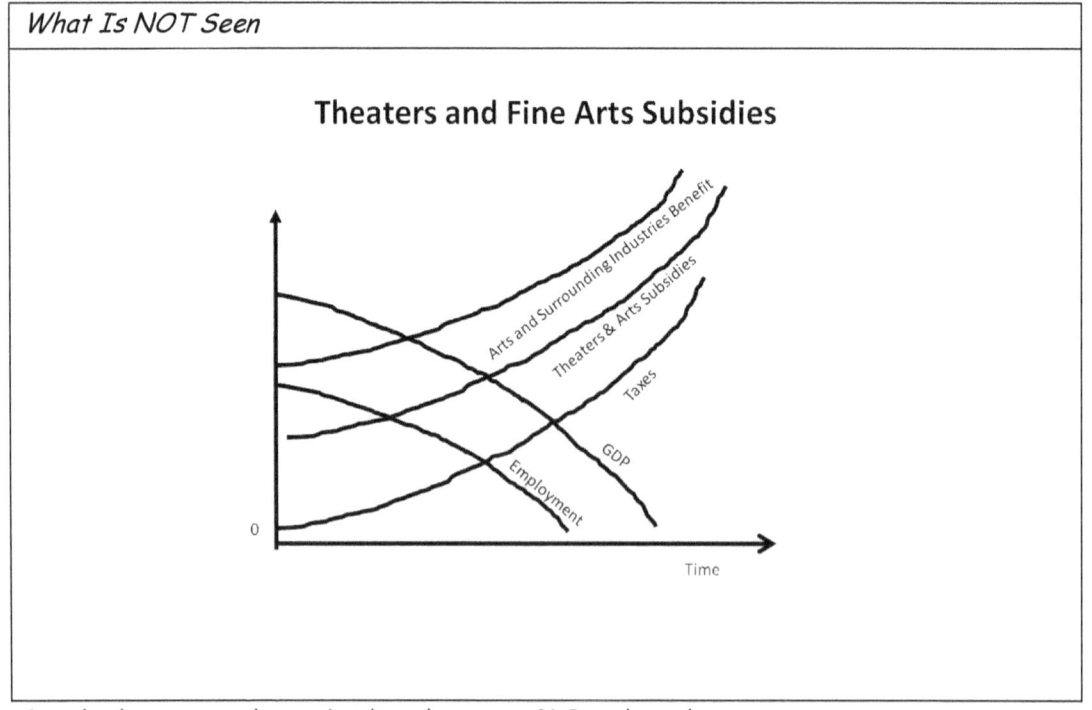

People see that subsidies increase benefit for the arts and its surrounding industries.

What Is NOT Seen

Theaters and Fine Arts Subsidies

People do not see that subsidies decrease GDP and employment.

Appendix: Learning Activities and Suggested Responses

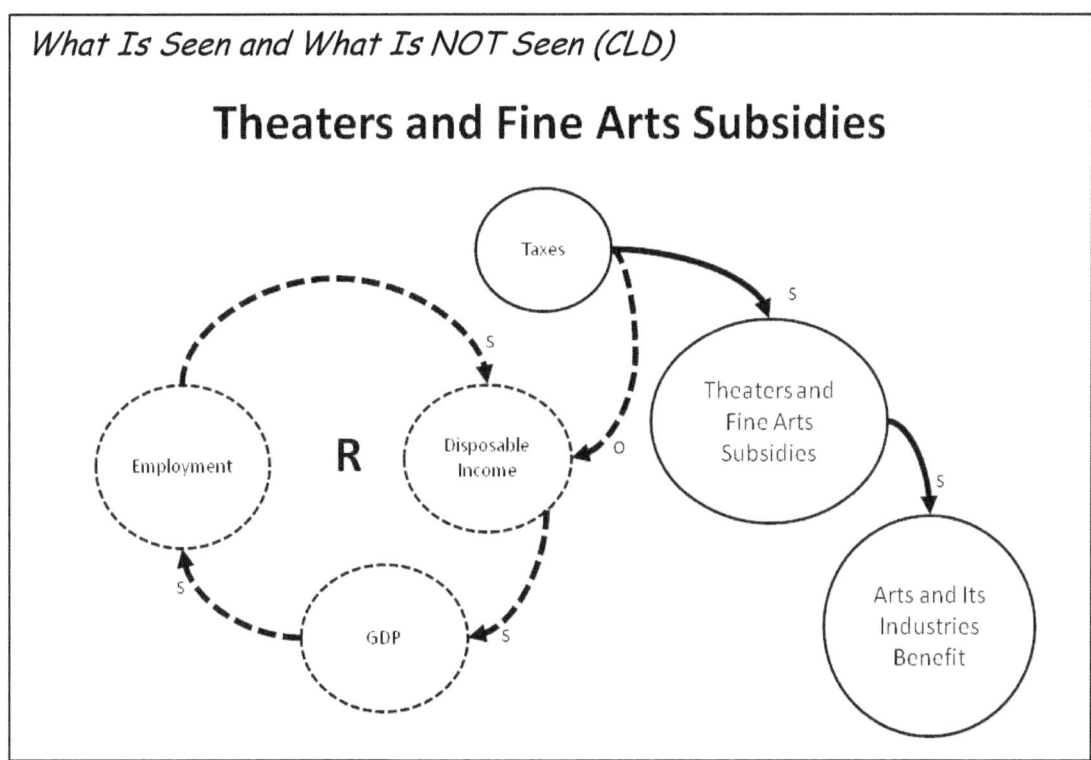

People see that subsidies go towards the arts and its surrounding industries. However, what people do not see is that taxes to pay for these subsidies decrease disposable income which in turn decreases GDP which in turn decreases employment and this then causes further declines in disposable income and GDP.

Hands-On Activity 1, Unit 5: Public Works

What Is Seen

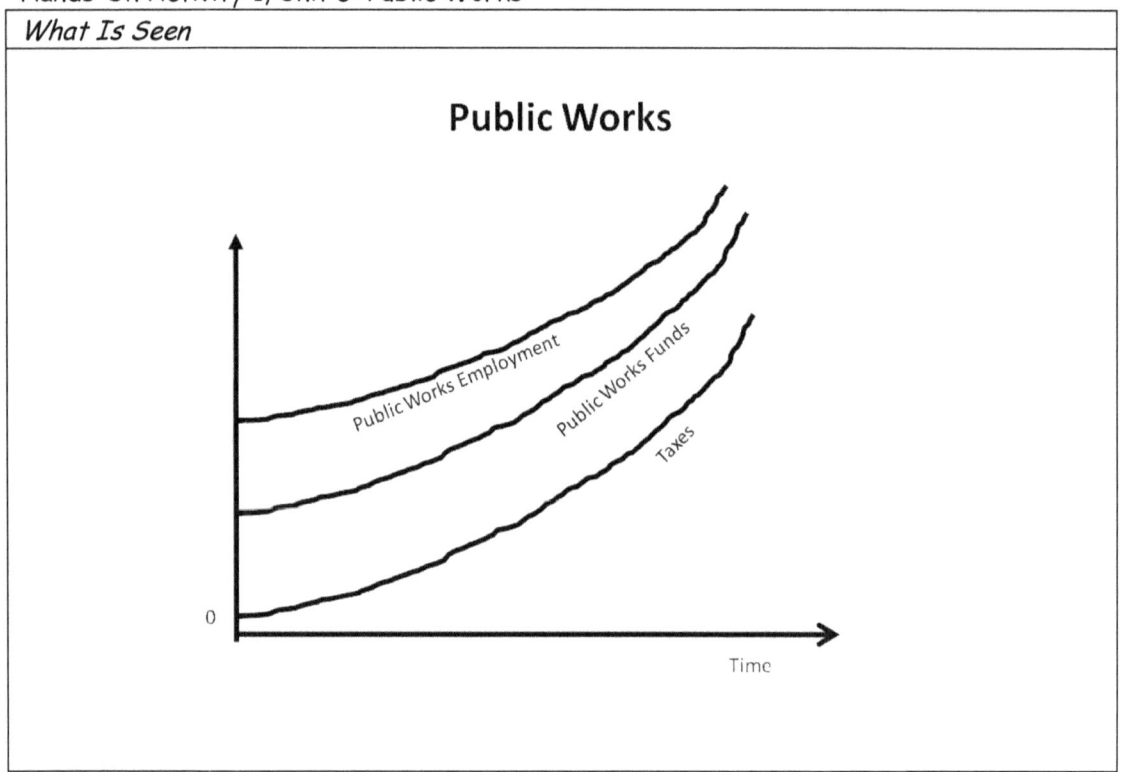

People see that taxes support public works funds which employ people directly involved in public works projects.

What Is NOT Seen

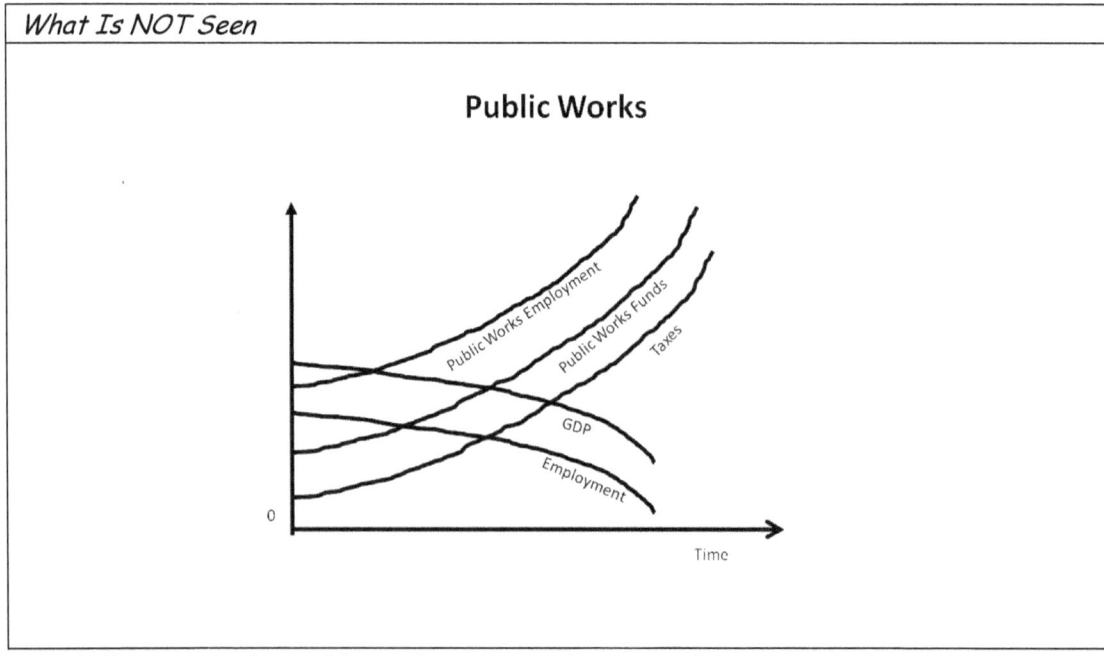

People do not see that public works projects decrease GDP and employment.

Appendix: Learning Activities and Suggested Responses

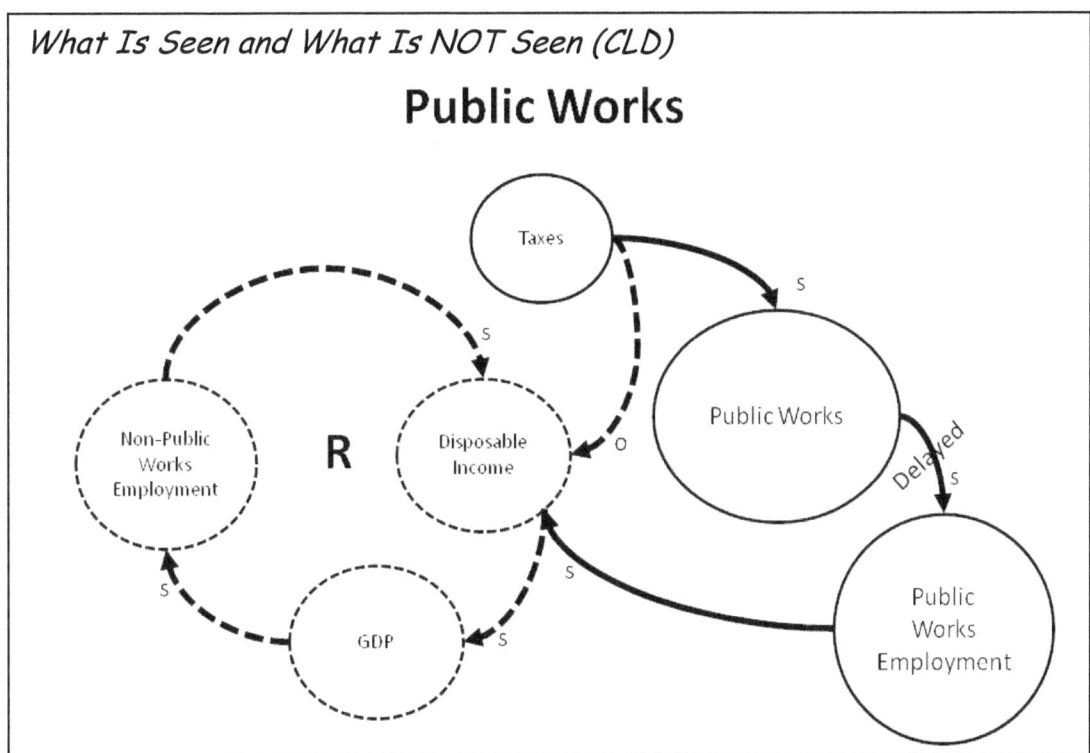

People see that public works create employment, but it is delayed employment that increases disposable income temporarily. People also see that these projects are short-term, such as bridge or road repairs. However, what people do not see is that taxes to pay for public works projects cause disposable income to decline overall which in turn decreases GDP which in turn decreases employment and this then causes further declines in disposable income and GDP.

Hands-On Activity 1, Unit 6: Middlemen

Free Market

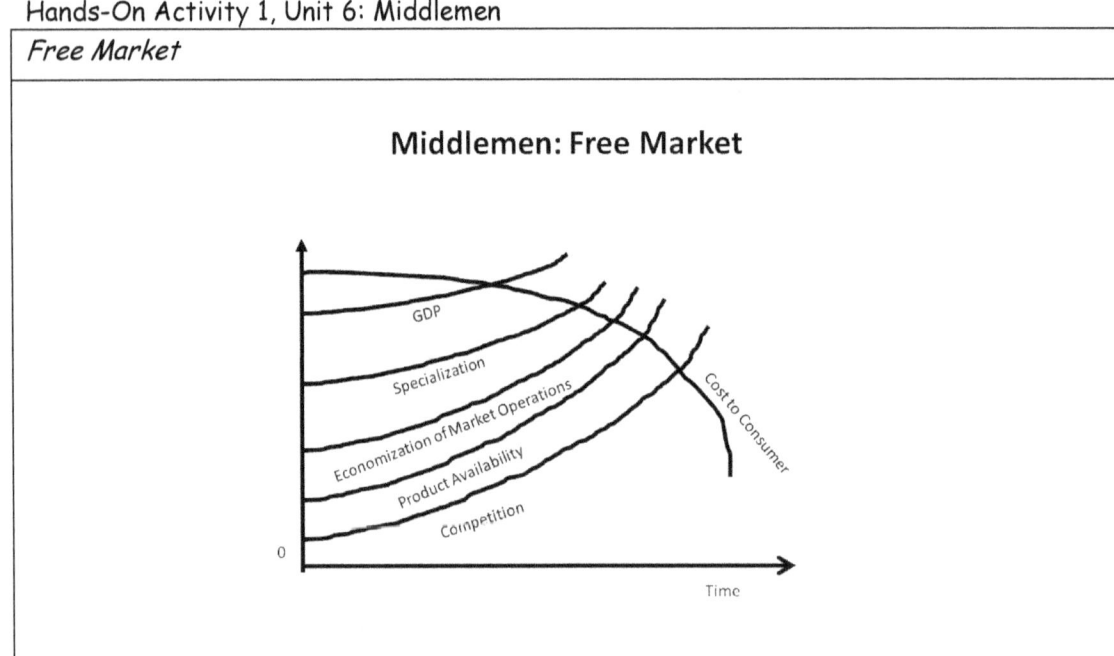

In a free market, competition increases product availability, economization of market operations, and specialization, which in turn decreases product costs to the consumer. As a result, GDP increases.

Nationalization

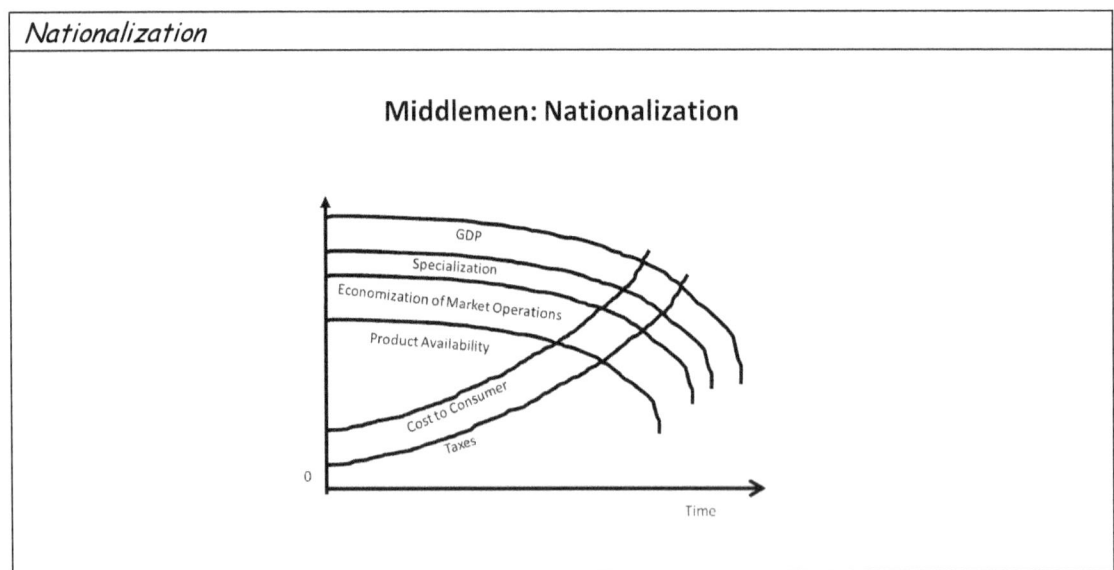

People do not see that nationalization increases taxes and product cost of consumers. In addition, product availability declines because competition has been eliminated or reduced. Furthermore, the profit incentive has been eliminated or reduced significantly; thus declining GDP.

Appendix: Learning Activities and Suggested Responses

What Is Seen and What Is NOT Seen (CLD 1): Free Market

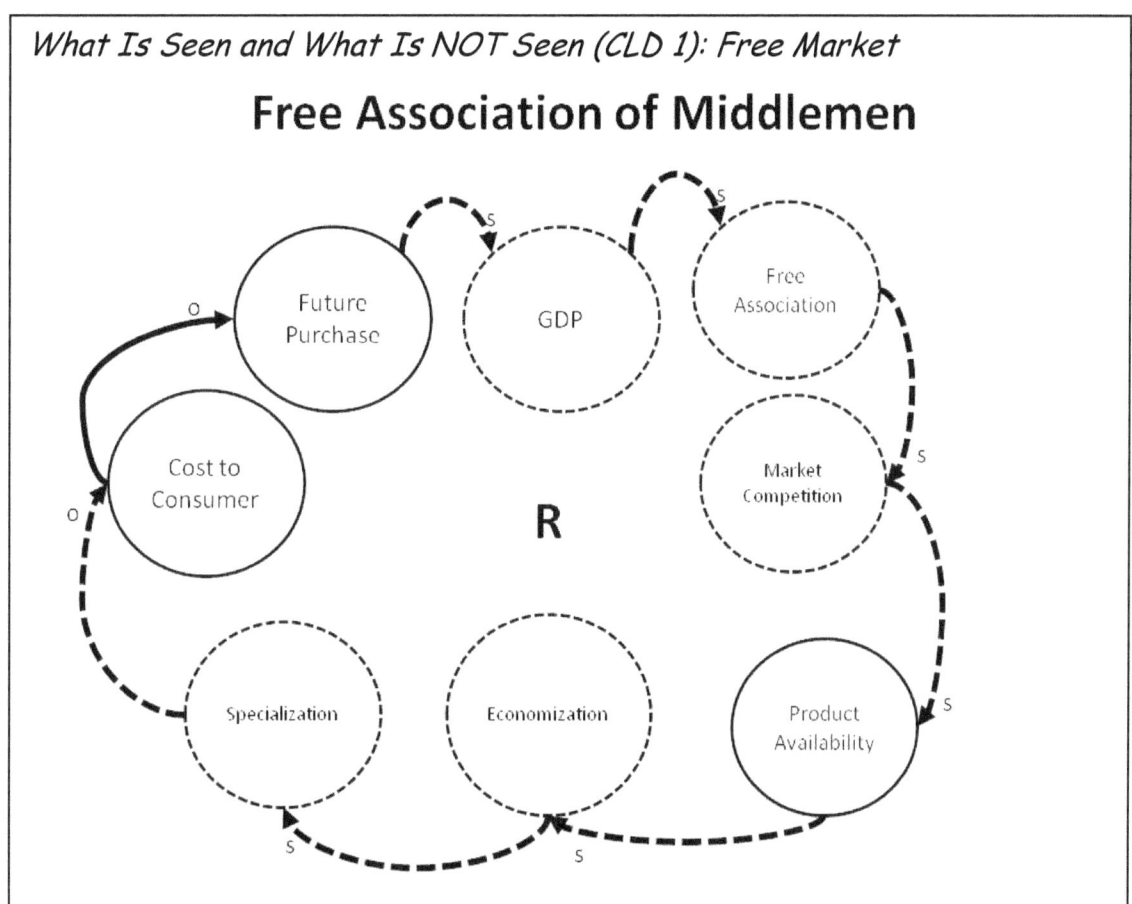

People only see product availability, the cost of products, and whether or not people are shopping. They do not see, however, all that is involved with free market activity when middlemen are allowed to associate freely. They do not see that free association increases market competition which in turn increases economization which in turn increases specialization which in turn decreases the cost to the consumer. They do not see that their future purchase increases GDP and spurs on further free association.

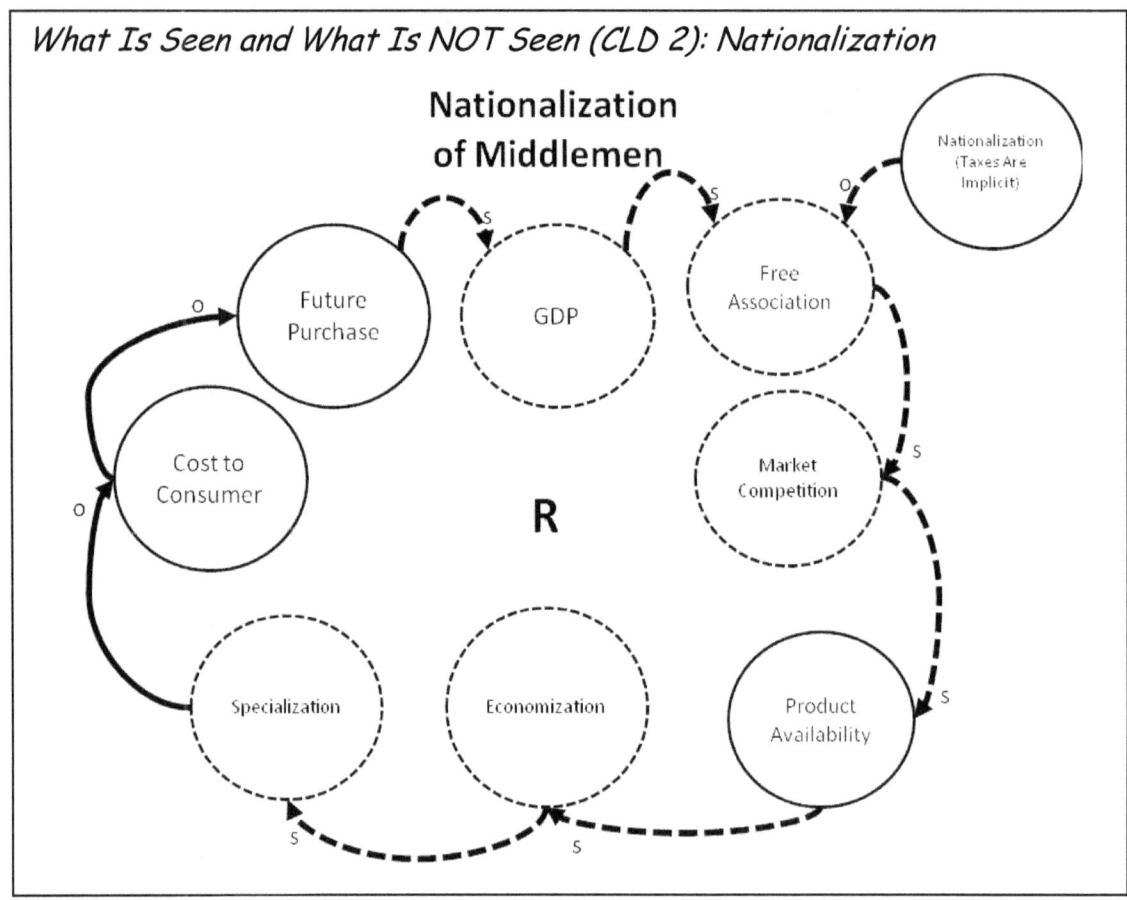

People only see product availability, the cost of products, and whether or not people are shopping. They do not see, however, all that is involved with nationalization when middlemen are no longer allowed to associate freely. They also forget that nationalization means an increase in taxes which in turn increases the product cost of consumers. In addition, they do not see that as a result of a decrease or elimination of competition that economization and specialization have been reduced or eliminated; thus causing a decline in GDP overall.

Hands-On Activity 1, Unit 7: Restraint of Trade

What Is Seen
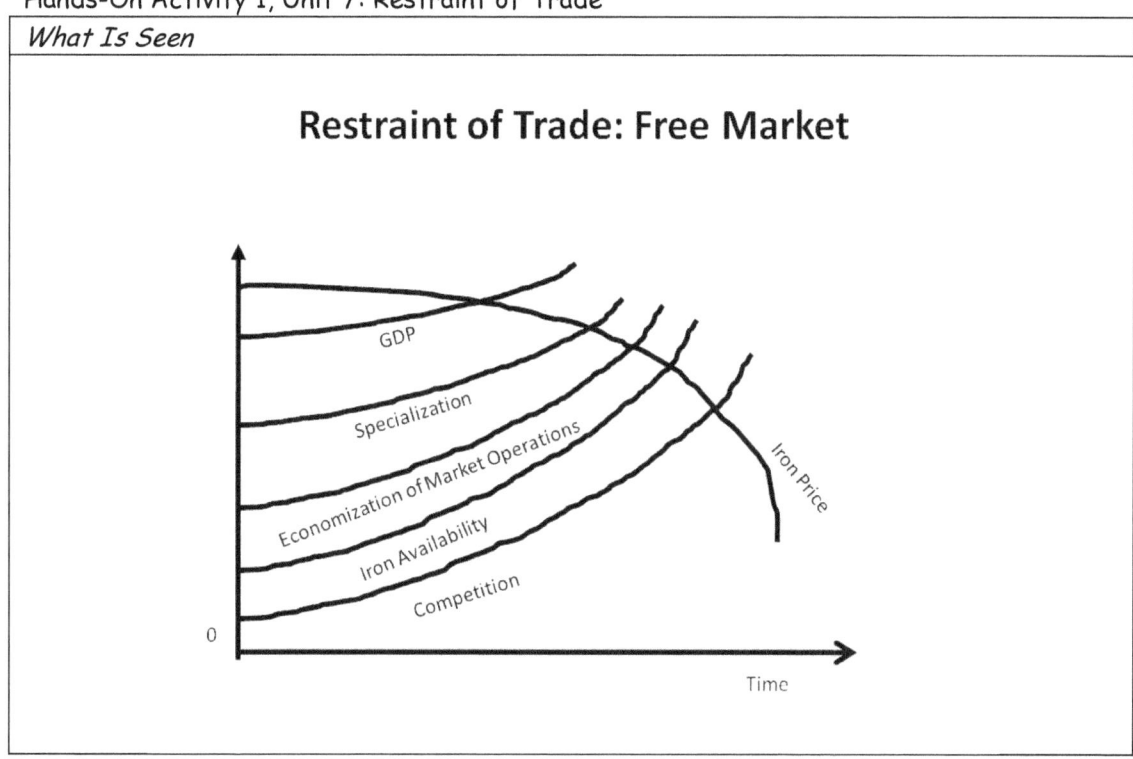

Free trade allows more competition and more iron availability which in turn increases economization which in turn increases specialization, and results in lower iron prices. This in turn increases GDP overall.

What Is NOT Seen
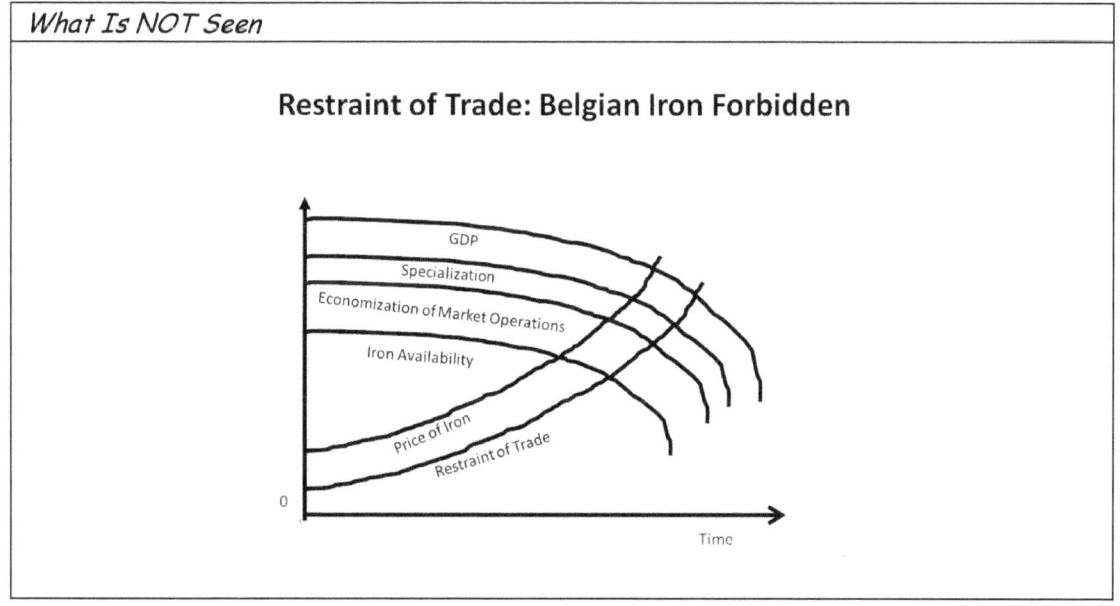

Restraint of trade causes the price of iron to increase as well as causes a decline in iron availability, economization, specialization, and GDP.

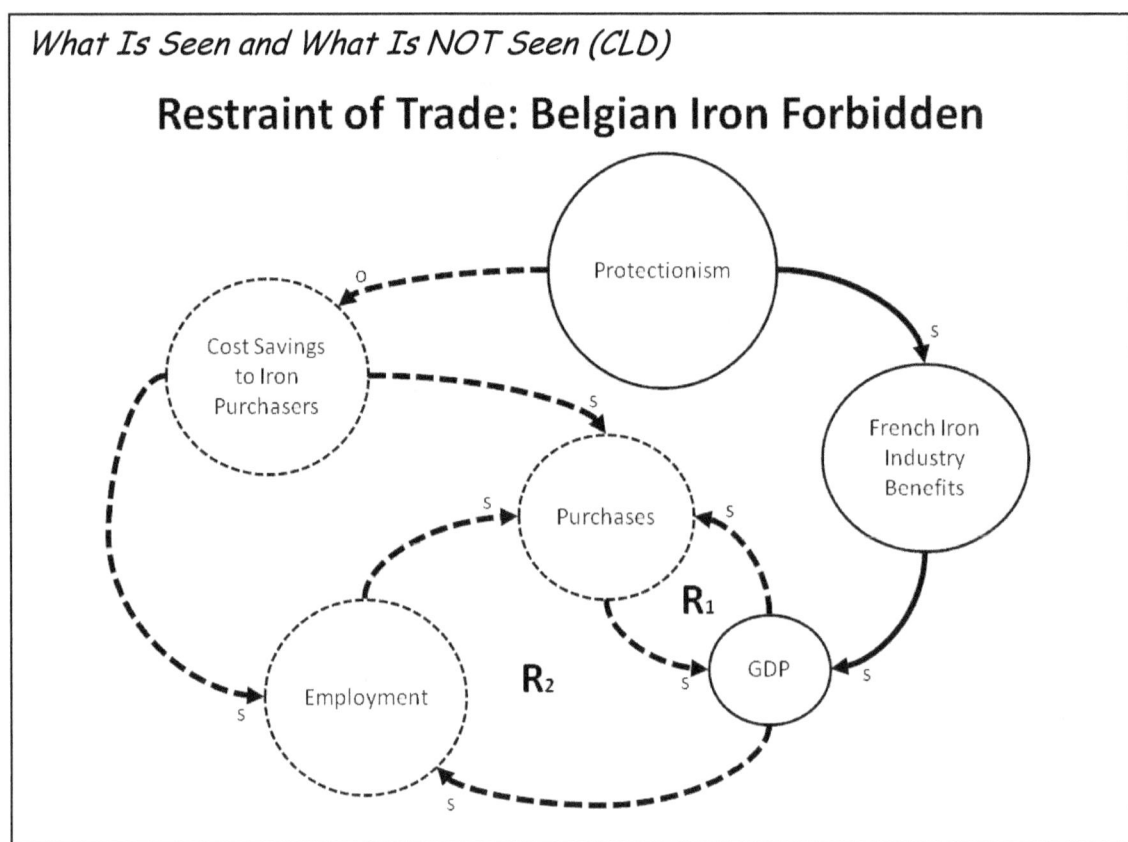

People see that the domestic iron industry gains from protectionism and assume that this is good for the entire economy. However, they do not see that restraint of trade is a net loss in GDP. The first loss is to the purchaser of iron since he now pays 5 francs more than before. The second loss is to the rest of the economy. The purchaser's cost savings of 5 francs goes toward domestic iron and away from non-iron sectors of the economy (R_1). For example, he could have purchased a book with his 5 francs; thus adding employment to this sector of the economy. Protectionists might say that employment is made up in the iron industry, but this is partially true. Diversification of an economy increases employment exponentially. The cost savings in iron increases the publishing sector by 5 francs, which in turn increases employment in another sector of the economy, such as the coffee business since writers drink a lot of coffee.

Now, if a nail company that employs 5,000 workers suddenly has to pay 5 francs more per iron purchase, then it will cut costs, such as lay off workers. This decline in employment causes greater decline in GDP (R_2); so any gains made in the iron industry will be exceeded by losses in other sectors of the economy.

Appendix: Learning Activities and Suggested Responses

Hands-On Activity 1, Unit 8: Machines

Technological Innovation in a Free Market

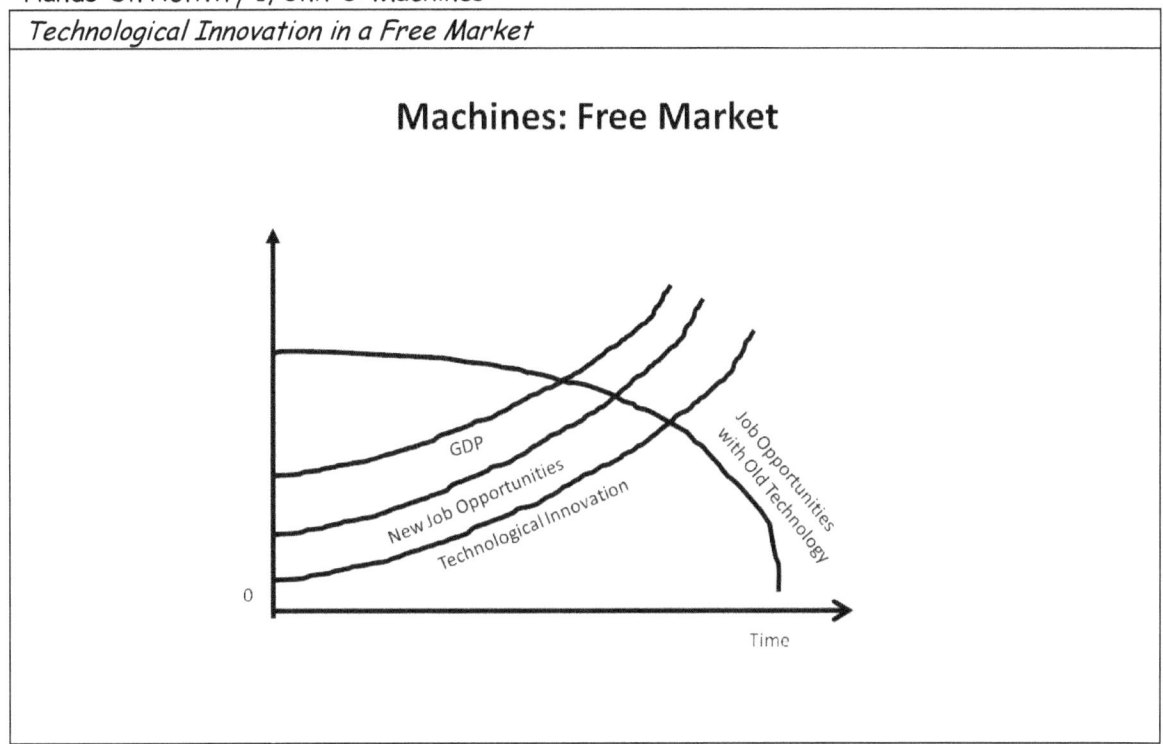

Technological innovation decreases job opportunities with old technology; however this is offset by new job opportunities created with new technology; thus increasing GDP.

Technology Restrained by Government

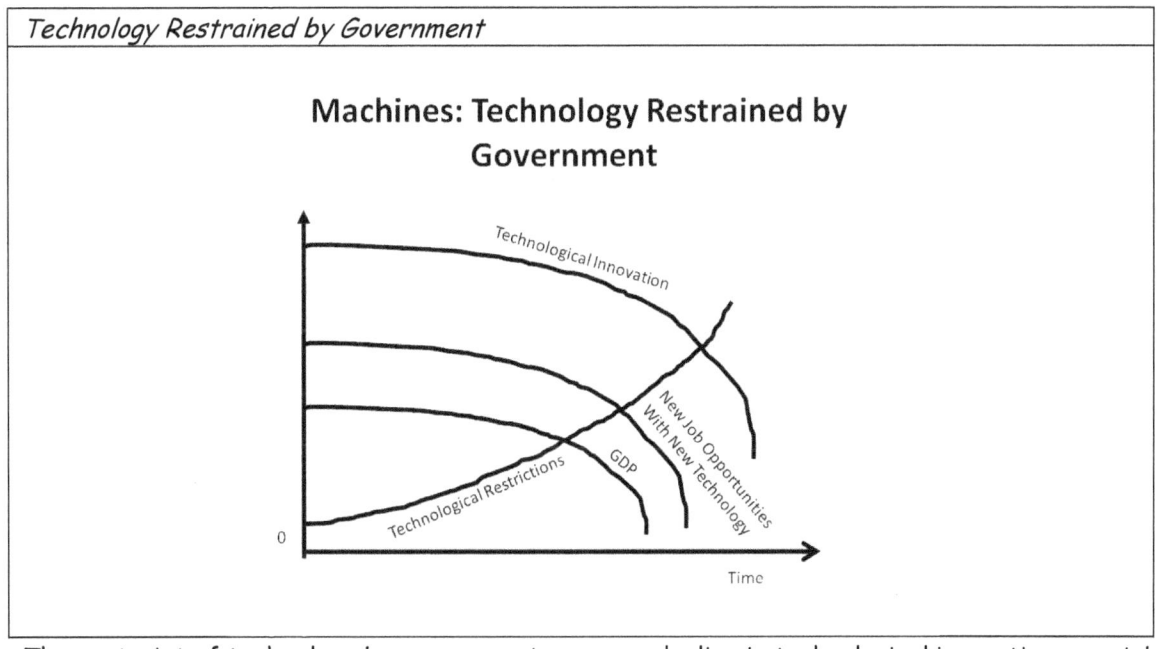

The restraint of technology by government causes a decline in technological innovation, new job opportunities with new technology, and finally GDP.

153

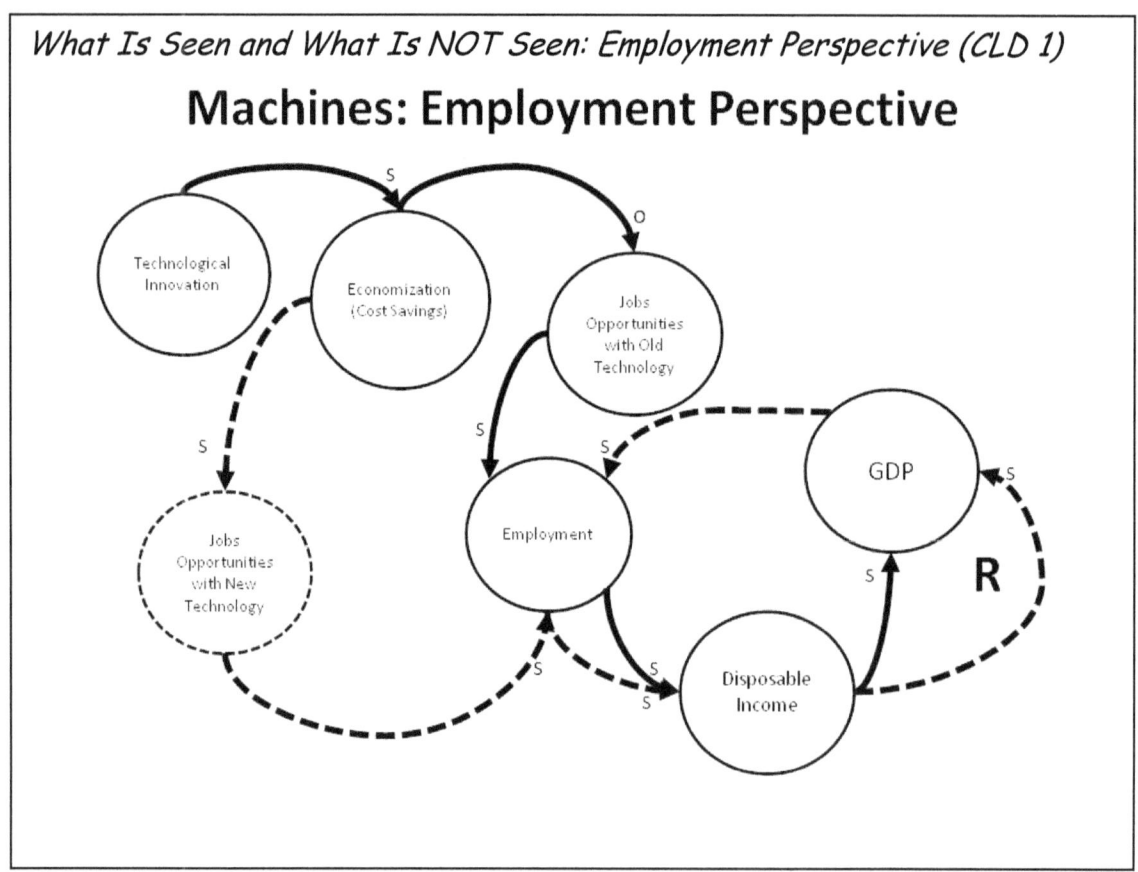

People see that technological innovation means jobs with the old technology are lost, such as the automobile replacing the horse and buggy. They rightly see the laid off people lose their disposable income and see GDP decline in the short-term. However, what they do not see is that new jobs are created as a result of the technological innovation and the laid off workers will find work in a new sector of the economy; thus increasing disposable income and GDP beyond that of which is initially lost in their lay off.

In addition, if government restrains technological innovation, it will, as Bastiat says, cause a society not to progress; thus, causing a decline in employment, disposable income, and GDP.

Appendix: Learning Activities and Suggested Responses

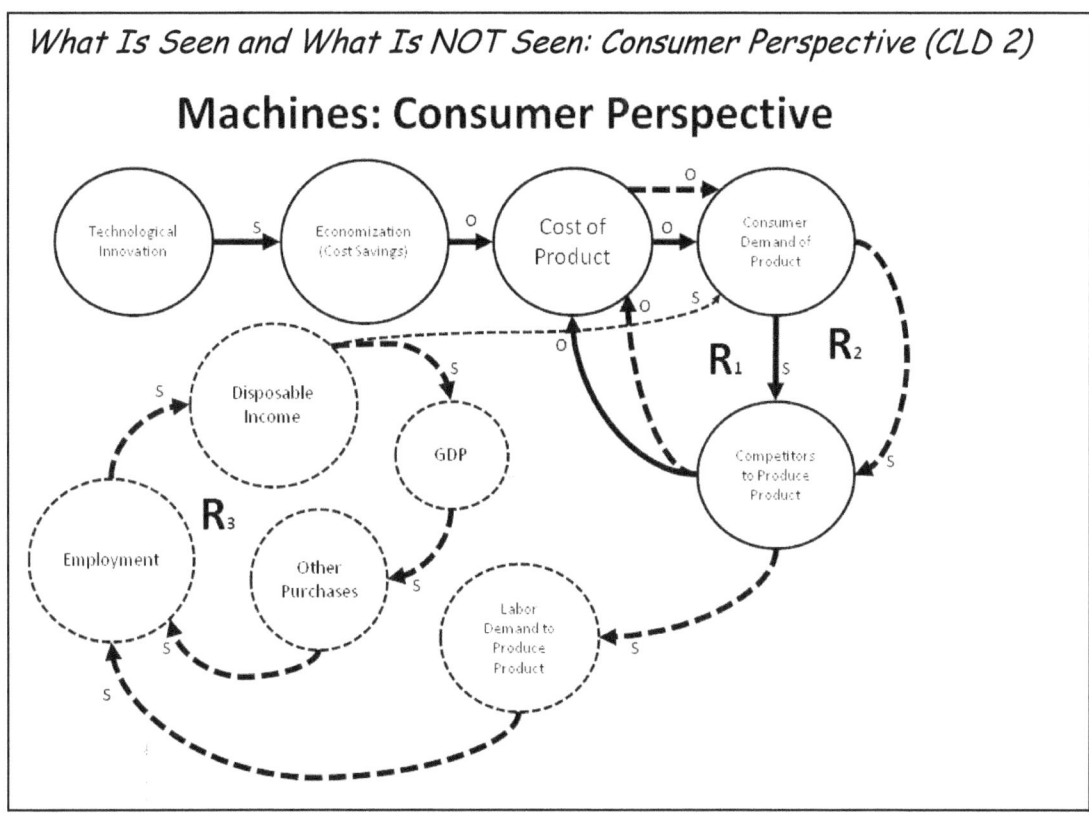

People see that an increase in technological innovation increases producer cost savings which in turn decreases product cost for the consumer. This lower product cost increases consumer demand for the product which in turn causes competitors to enter the market to produce the product. This in turn lowers the cost of the product for the consumer even more (R_1).

Furthermore, with competitors in the market, the labor demand to produce the product increases. This increase in labor demand increases employment which then increases disposable income. This disposable income may be spent in two ways: to buy more of the current product (R_2) or buy other products in the economy (R_3). Either way, the GDP increases.

However, if technological innovation is restrained, we see an increase in product cost, a decline in consumer demand, and a decline in the number of competitors wanting to produce it. This in turn causes employment, disposable income, and GDP to decline. As Bastiat says, society becomes stagnant.

Hands-On Activity 1, Unit 9: Credit

What Is Seen

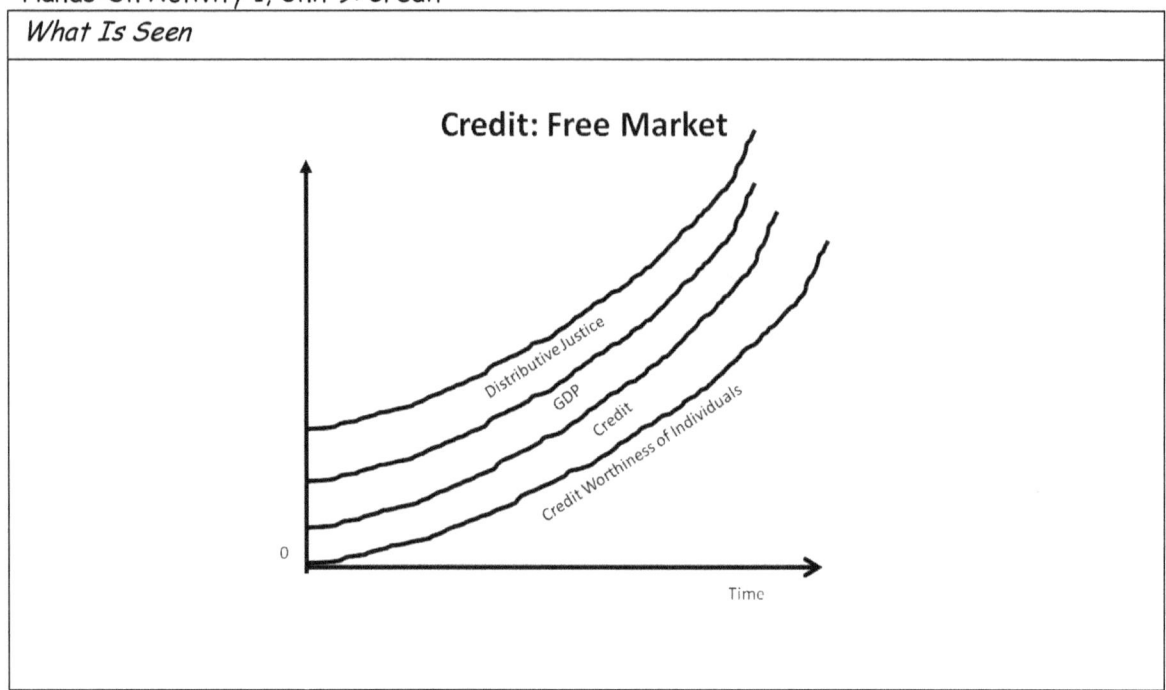

People see that credit worthy people receive loans which in turn increases credit which then increases GDP and distributive justice.

What Is NOT Seen

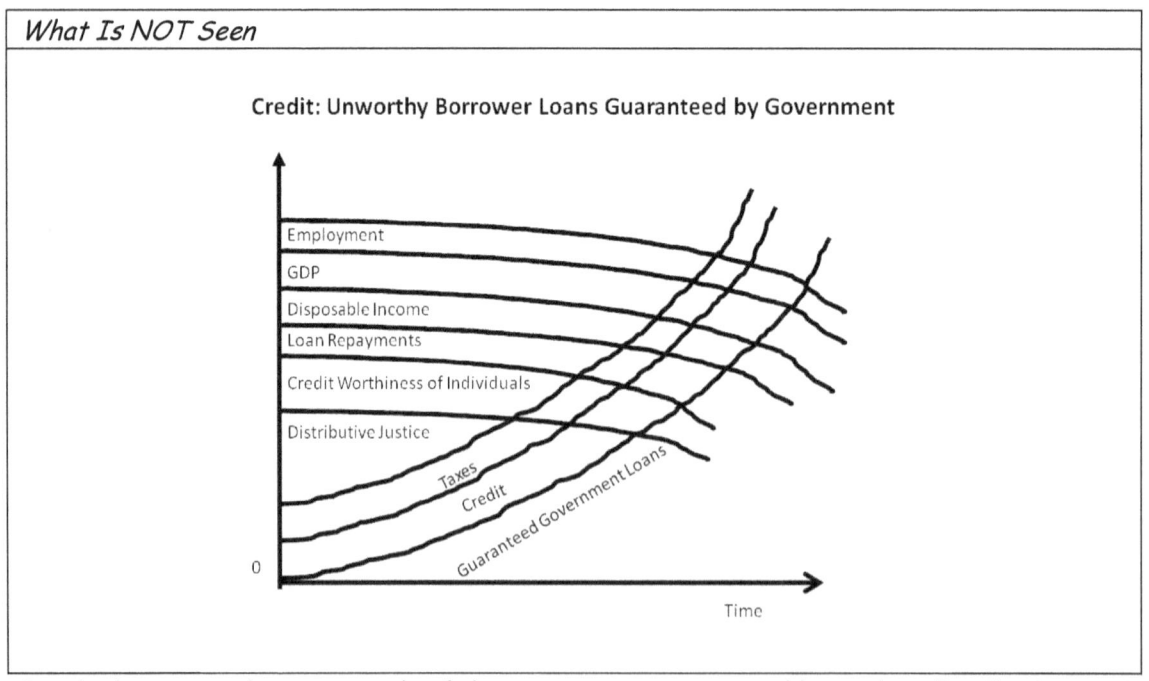

People do not see that as a result of the government guaranteed loans that distributive justice has been deprived of credit worthy individuals and taxpayers and that the result is a decline in GDP and employment.

Appendix: Learning Activities and Suggested Responses

What Is Seen and What Is NOT Seen: Government Guaranteed Loans (CLD)

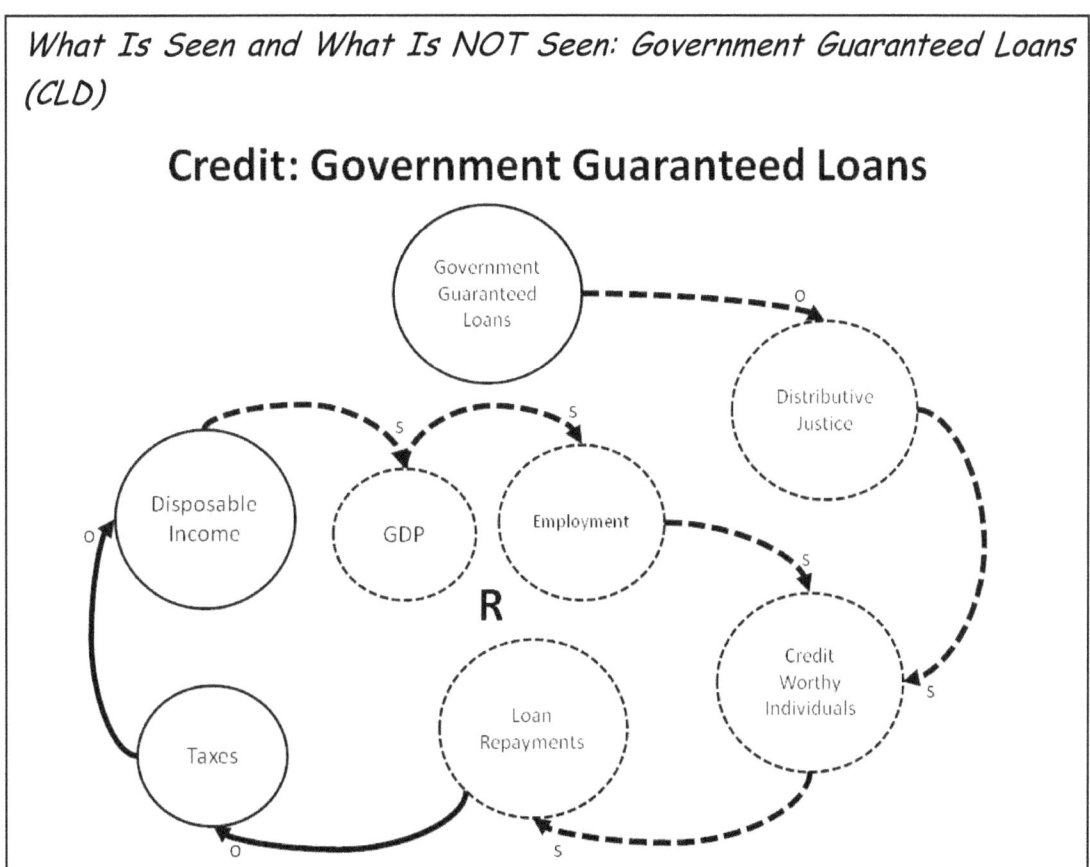

An increase in government guaranteed loans decreases distributive justice. Distributive justice is respect for the human person and the rights which flow from human dignity and guarantee it. More specifically, society must provide the conditions that allow people to obtain what is their due, according to their nature and their vocation. As Bastiat states, these are life, liberty, and property. In the case of John the farmer, we saw that his and the taxpayer's human dignity had been violated by government. Therefore, a decline in distributive justice causes a decline in credit worthy individuals because this enforces a psychology that says, "If the government violates my human dignity by awarding others what is my due, then what is my incentive for doing good? What the heck, if the government is guaranteeing my loan, then why should I even worry about paying it back?" As a result, loan repayments decline, taxes increase "to bail out the bums," and taxpayer disposable income also declines. This causes GDP to decline which in turn causes employment to decline and exasperates a decline in credit worthy individuals.

Hands-On Activity 1, Unit 10: Algeria

What Is Seen
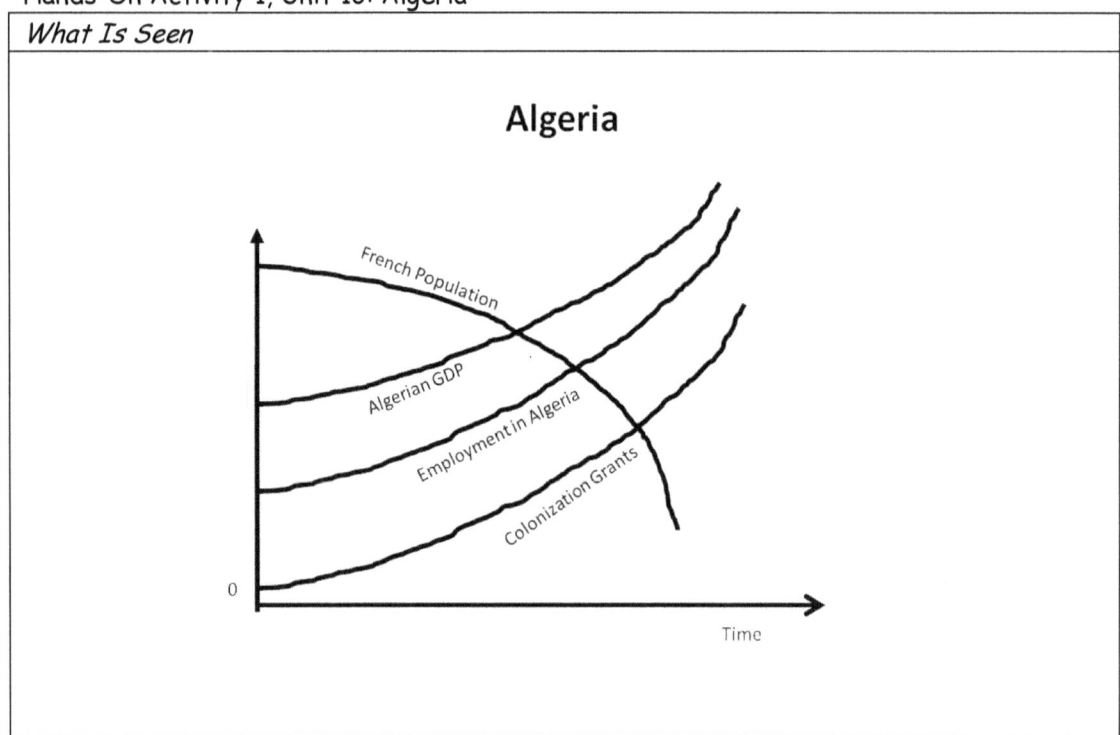

People see that colonization grants increase employment in Algeria and Algerian GDP. They also see a decline in the French population.

What Is NOT Seen
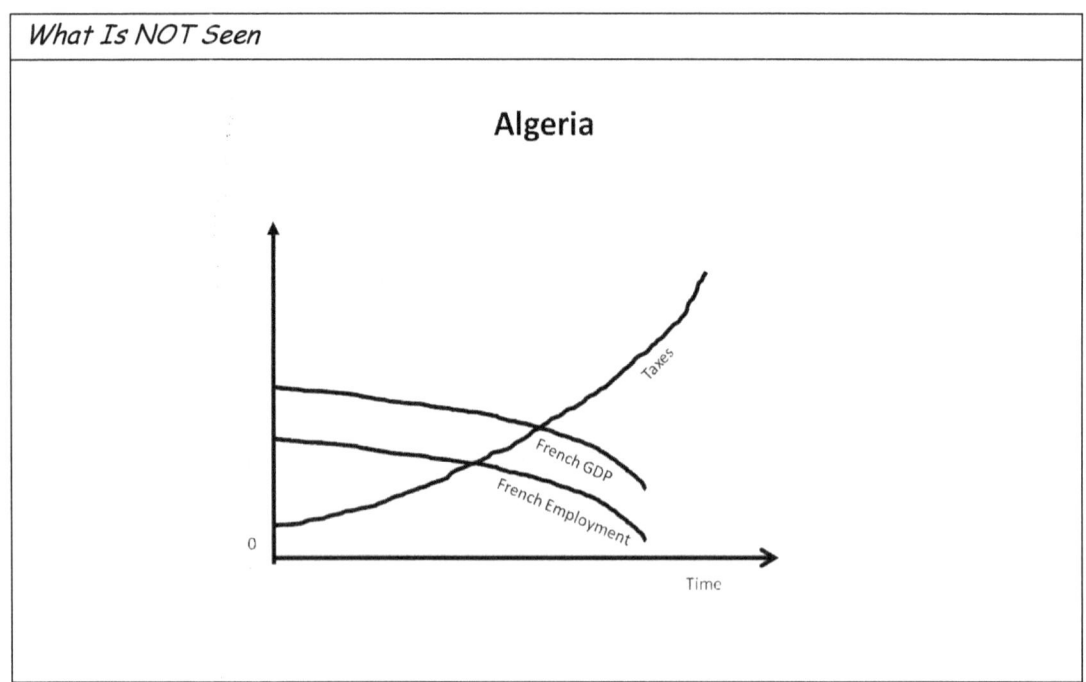

People do not see that colonization grants increase taxes and decrease GDP and employment in France.

Appendix: Learning Activities and Suggested Responses

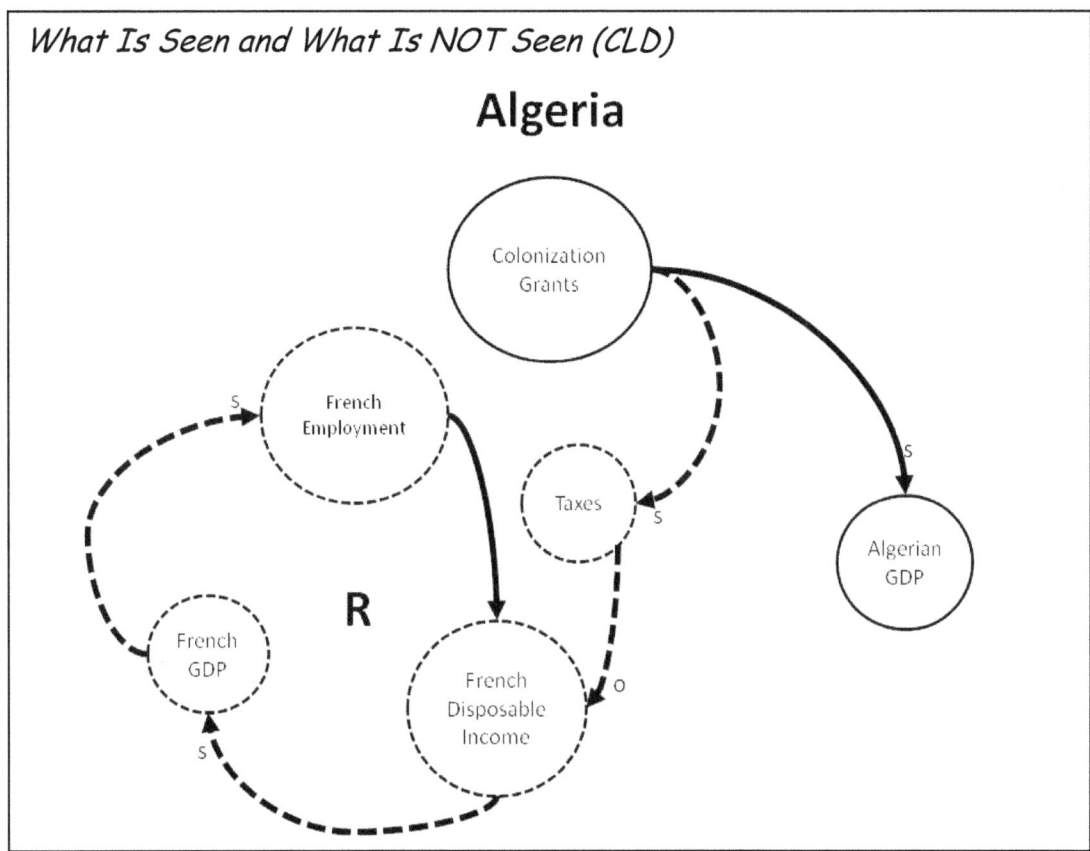

People see that colonization grants increase the GDP of Algeria. However, what they do not see is that to pay for these grants taxes must be increased in France. This causes French disposable income to decline which in turn causes French GDP to decline which then causes French employment to decline causing a further decline in French disposable income.

Hands-On Activity 1, Unit 11: Thrift and Luxury

What Is Seen
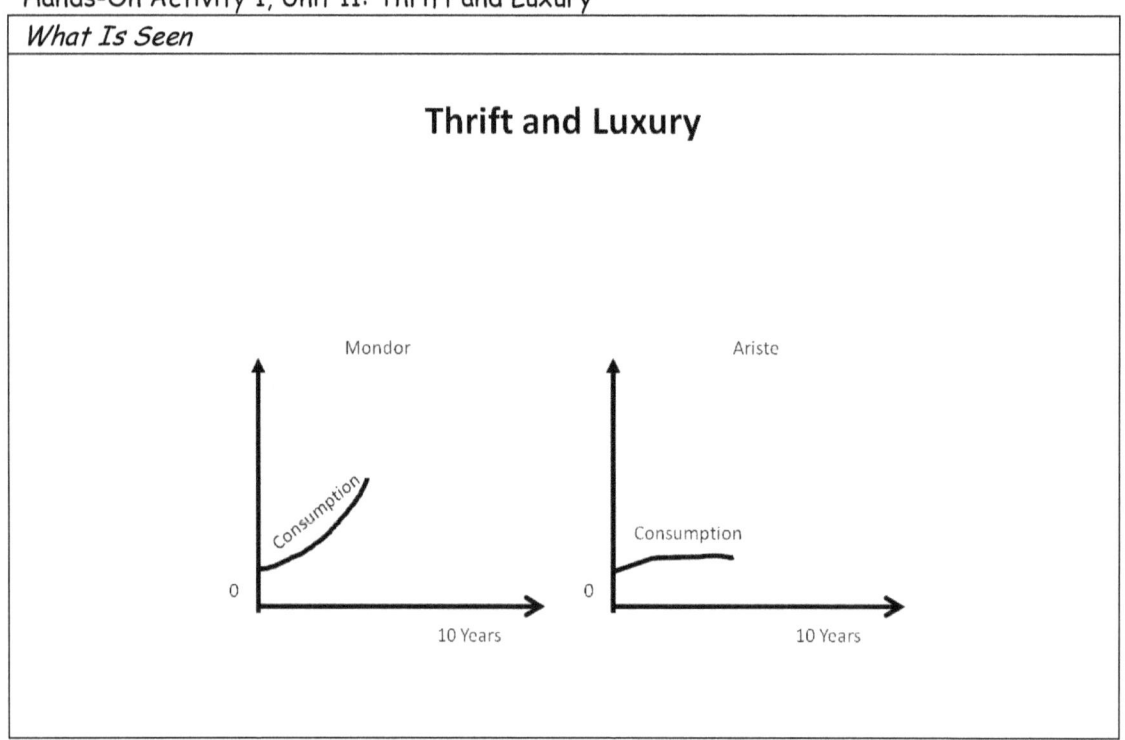

People see that Mondor spends more money than Ariste.

What Is NOT Seen
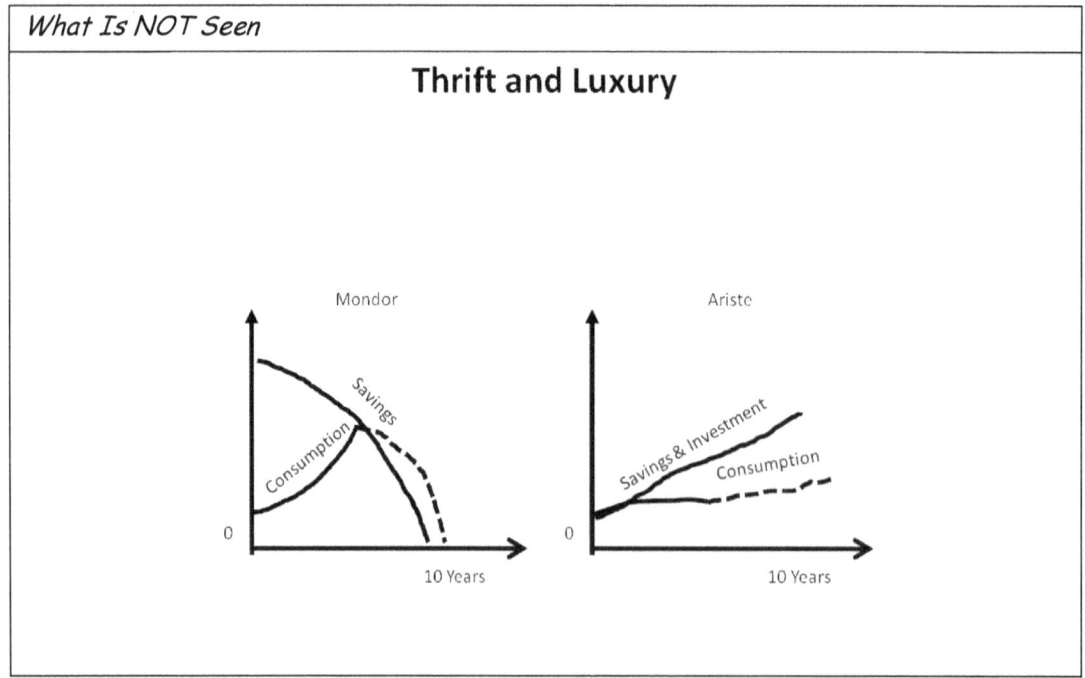

People do not see that Mondor's savings rate is zero and that his consumption will also be zero at the end of ten years. They also do not see that Ariste saves and invests which maintains his consumption far beyond the ten years.

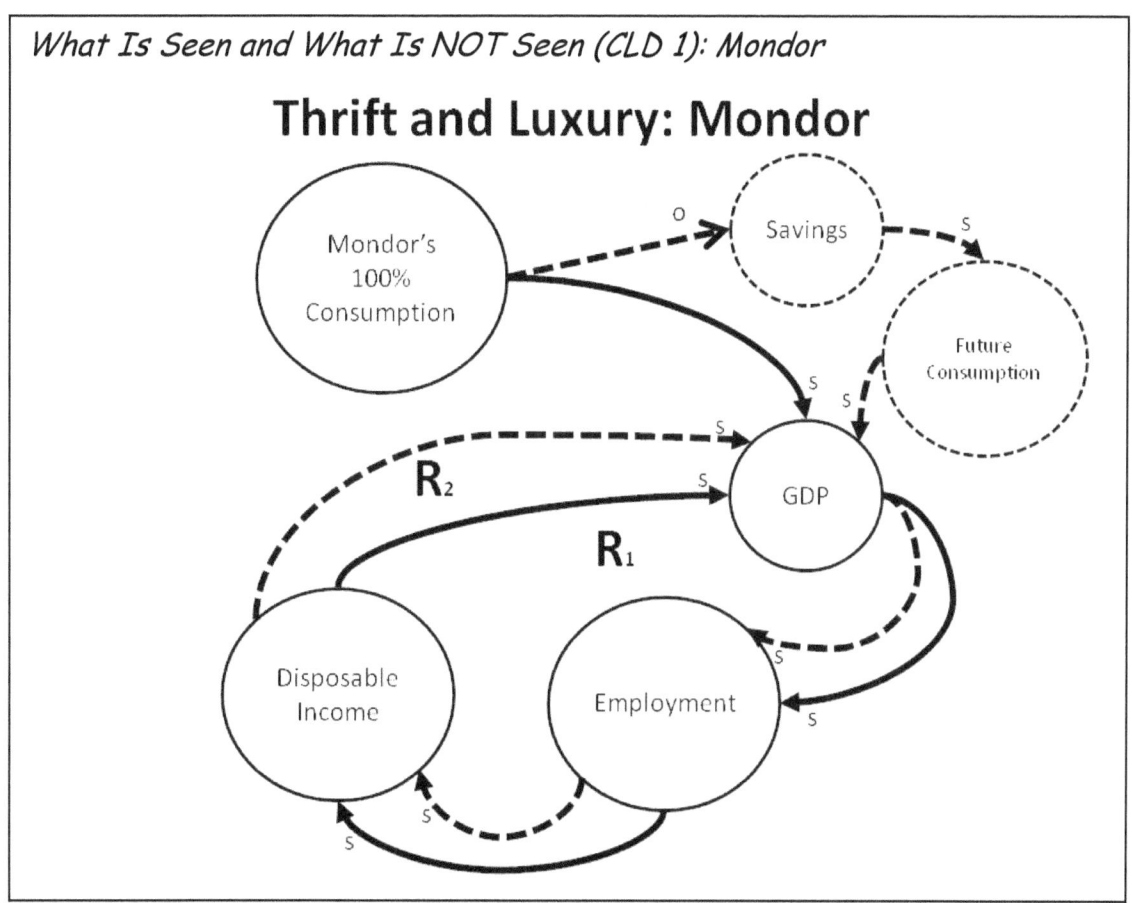

People see that Mondor spends money like crazy and that it increases GDP (R_1). However, what they do not see is that Mondor does not save any of his money and this causes a decline in future consumption which in turn causes a decline in future GDP (R_2).

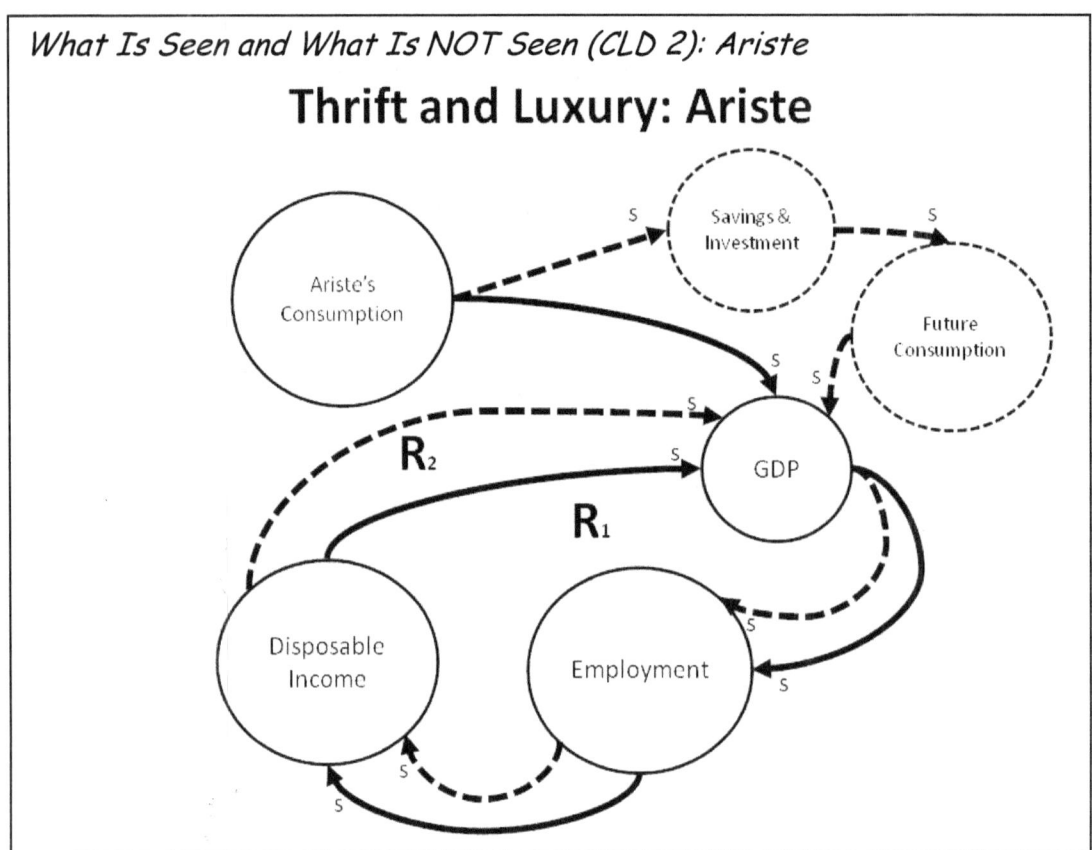

People see that Ariste does not spend as much money as Mondor and think he is stingy (R_1). However, what they do not see is that Ariste saves and invests and this will increase GDP over the long-term (R_2).

Appendix: Learning Activities and Suggested Responses

Hands-On Activity 1, Unit 12: The Right to Employment and the Right to Profit

What Is Seen

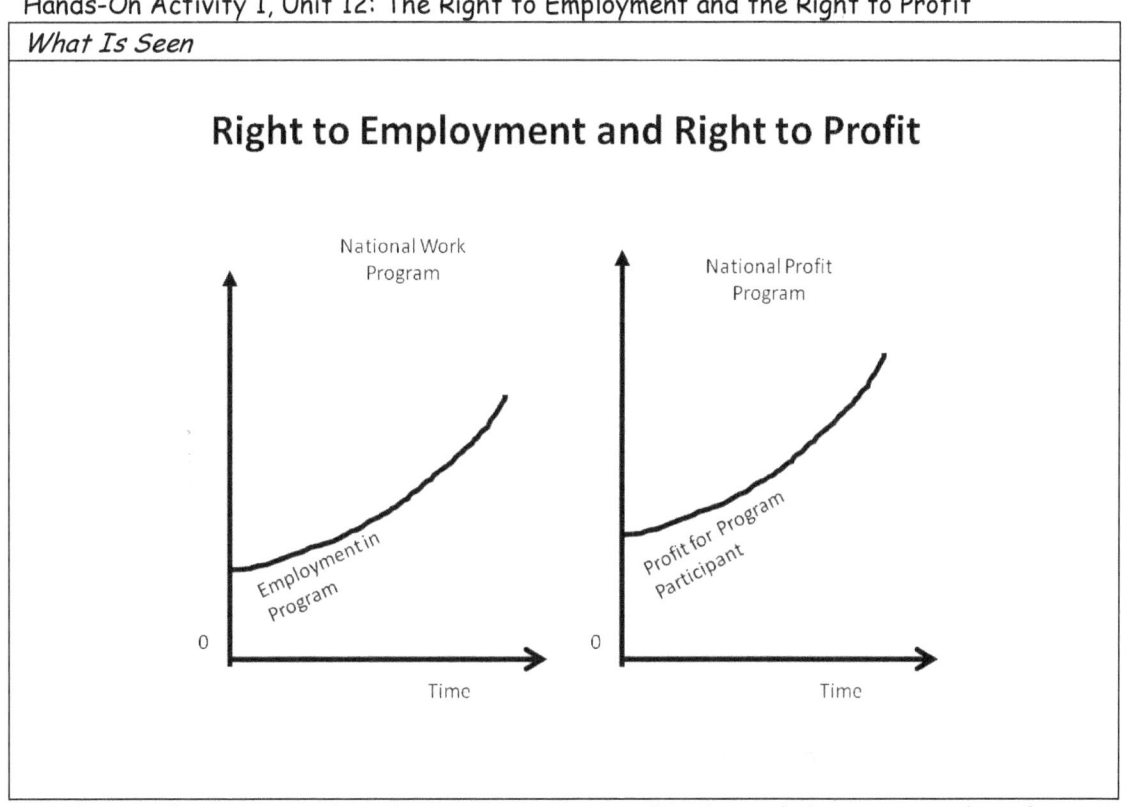

People see that a national work program gives people jobs and that a national profit program subsidizes the losses of a company.

What Is NOT Seen

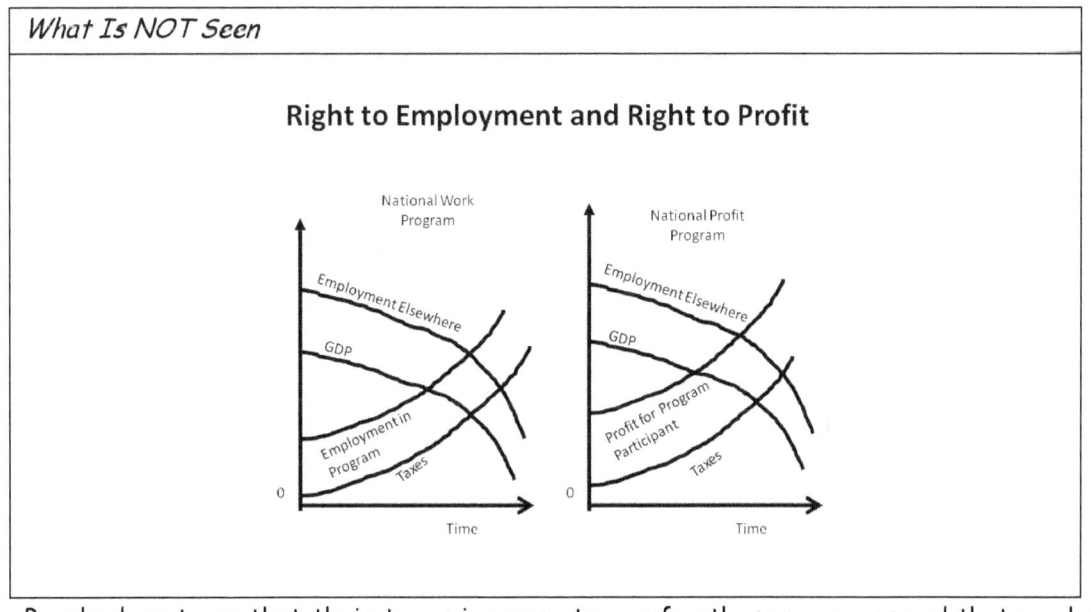

People do not see that their taxes increase to pay for these programs and that employment elsewhere as well as GDP decline.

163

What Is Seen and What Is Not Seen: Fun Systems Thinking Activities with Frédéric Bastiat

What Is Seen and What Is NOT Seen: Government Right to Employment and Profit Programs (CLD)

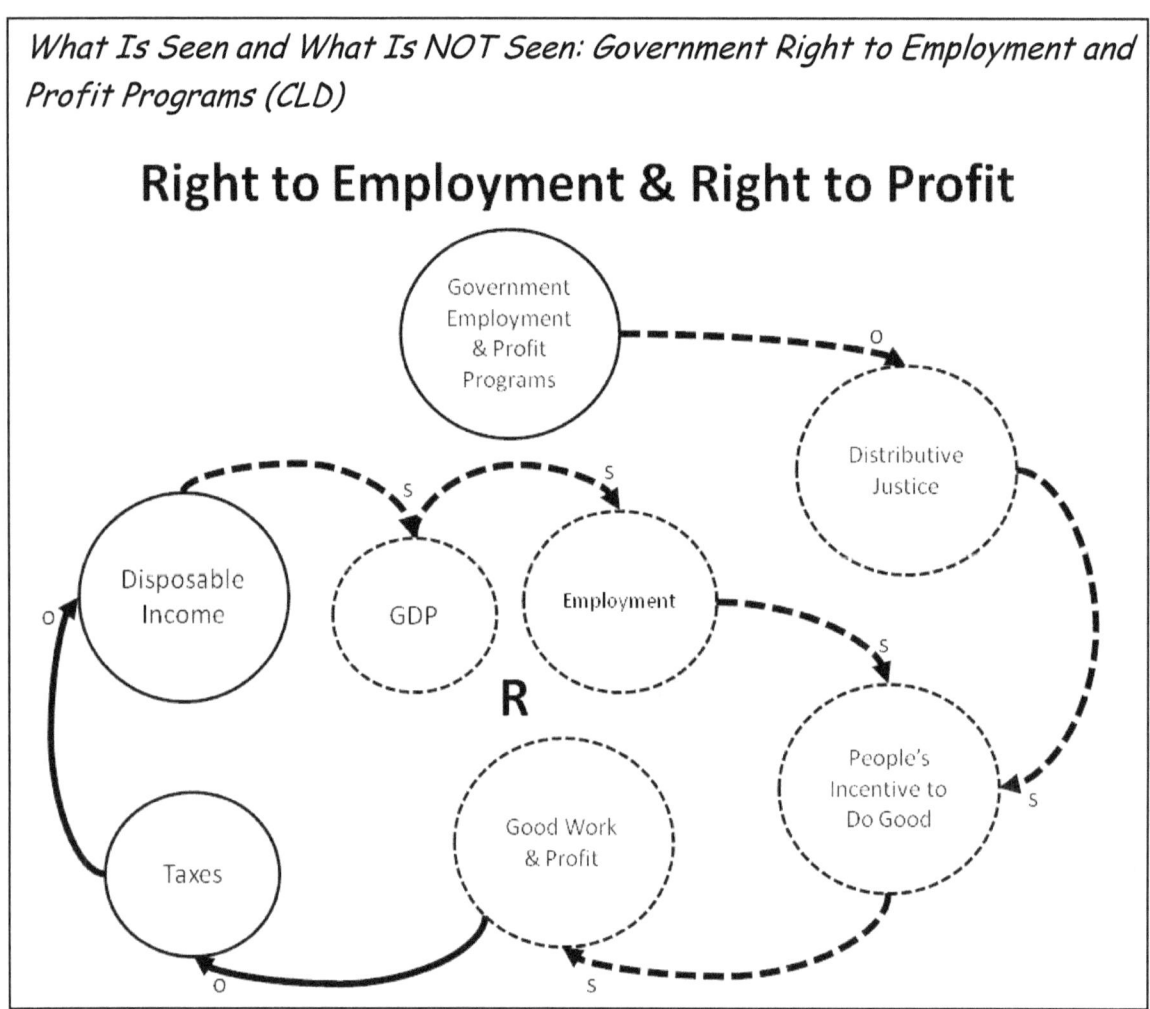

This is similar to the situation in Unit 9 regarding government guaranteed loans. An increase in government employment and profit programs decreases distributive justice. Therefore, a decline in distributive justice causes a decline in people's incentive to do good work in society. It enforces a psychology that says, "If the government violates my human dignity by awarding others what is my due, then what is my incentive for doing good? What the heck, if the government is covering another company's losses or finding jobs for other people, then why should I even worry about making a profit or looking for work or doing a good job where I work now?" As a result, good work and profits decline, taxes increase "to bail out the bums," and taxpayer disposable income also declines. This causes GDP to decline which in turn causes employment to decline and exasperates a decline in individual responsibility in society.

www.ingramcontent.com/pod-product-compliance
Lightning Source LLC
Chambersburg PA
CBHW082121230426
43671CB00015B/2769